A School Leader's Guide to Reclaiming Purpose

A School Leader's Guide to Reclaiming Purpose

Frederick C. Buskey

ConnectEDD Publishing
Hanover, Pennsylvania

This publication is available at discount pricing when purchased in quantity for educational purposes, promotions, or fundraisers. For inquiries and details, contact the publisher at: info@connecteddpublishing.com

Published by ConnectEDD Publishing LLC
Hanover, PA
www.connecteddpublishing.com

Cover Design: Kheila Casas

A School Leader's Guide to Reclaiming Purpose by Frederick C. Buskey. —1st ed. Paperback ISBN 979-8-9890027-1-9

ConnectEDD

PUBLISHING

Praise for *A School Leader's Guide to Reclaiming Purpose*

Those new to school administration as well as veteran school leaders will find value in *A School Leader's Guide to Reclaiming Purpose*. In this guide to leading successfully, Dr. Buskey presents a format that will support school leaders as they identify purposeful processes needed to lead in a modern school setting. The format used allows for realistic timelines and encourages collaboration in what is often an overwhelming and solitary profession. Individual school leaders as well as district leadership teams will find value and professional purpose in implementing this guide.

> —Dr. Sam Sircey | Associate Dean of Academics and Student Services, South College, Secondary School Principal, retired

I am delighted to have met and exchanged important ideas with Frederick. He is committed to helping school leaders support their teachers. I can't imagine a more critical focus, and I can't imagine a more capable force than Frederick. I am better because of him, and in reading his book, you will be better, too.

> —Lisa Perry, M. Ed. | PK-12 Principal, AP Lang & Comp Teacher, Curriculum Director

Hats off to Dr. Frederick Buskey for creating a survival guide like this for school leaders! Use the practices and advice in this book as your personal handbook. Not only may this resource prevent more leaders from leaving the profession, but more importantly, may it provide you space and permission to find joy and satisfaction by expanding your capacity for helping students, supporting teachers, and reaching communities. Well done!

> —William D. Parker | Founder of Principal Matters: Education Leadership Services

Dr. Frederick Buskey has created a blueprinted masterpiece that all educational leaders need to read. His work is a practical, yet necessary examination of work/life balance in the ever increasingly responsible world of school leadership. Professional progress without purpose, may not be personally profitable! I highly recommend this addition to your library, whether the reader is at the beginning or midst of an educational leadership journey!

—William T. Wright, Jr., Ed.D. | Superintendent, Sumter School District, South Carolina

This book exposes the urgency trap and offers tools to reclaim the core: fostering a thriving school community built on well-being, teacher empowerment, and strong student connections. It unveils an essential truth: prioritizing students starts with supporting teachers. Creating a culture of mutual respect and care unlocks transformative learning. Leaders who embrace presence empower themselves and cultivate an environment where everyone thrives. This guide ignites the soul of education, offering invaluable insights for leaders driving positive change.

—Dr. Efraín Martínez | Principal and podcaster

So many leaders enter school administration in a sprint, not realizing leadership is a long game in which one can easily lose life balance and direction with the numerous responsibilities under their charge. Frederick Buskey's guide provides content and scenarios in which leaders learn to better prioritize and strategize as they deepen their understanding of self. This guide is a gift for those who will take the time to invest in themselves as they read, analyze, reflect, and find their own pace in order to run a long, successful leadership race.

—Dr. Heidi Von Dohlen | Associate Professor and Program Director, Western Carolina University

In *A School Leader's Guide to Reclaiming Purpose*, Dr. Buskey skillfully addresses the common challenges encountered by school leaders, offering a practical and conceptual framework for achieving meaningful engagement. As a dedicated EduReader, I often encounter repetitive content laden with trendy jargon. Yet, Dr. Buskey's authentic experiences breathe fresh insight into the complexities of leadership, striking a balance between validation and simplification.

—Maria Werner | Principal GREEN Charter School Simpsonville

A School Leader's Guide to Reclaiming Purpose by Frederick Buskey is a transformative tool that empowers leaders to evolve at their own pace. Buskey's approach, rooted in naturalistic learning, allows for personalized growth and mastery. Whether you choose to embark on the journey solo, with a partner, or as part of a group study, this guide accommodates diverse learning preferences. With practical advice and structured frameworks, Buskey ensures that every stage of the leadership journey is navigated with clarity and intention from a genuine place of support of guidance. Think of Reclaiming Purpose as your specifically tailored accountability partner on the path to success and embrace this invaluable resource to reclaim your purpose and unlock your full potential as a leader!

—Dr. Mary Hemphill | CEO & Founder of *The Limitless Leader*

Frederick Buskey's *A School Leader's Guide to Reclaiming Purpose* emerges as a pivotal read for education leaders navigating the complexities of modern schooling. With an insightful lens on alignment, Buskey adeptly identifies the crux of educational challenges—misalignment within purpose, resources, structures, and capabilities. This guide transcends conventional leadership advice, offering a structured approach to diagnosing and rectifying discord in school systems. Particularly compelling is the exploration of the "Three Epiphanies," which reframes the daunting task of educational leadership into manageable, value-driven choices. Buskey's narrative is not just a call to action but a roadmap for principals and school leaders striving for emotional safety, purposeful direction, and impactful leadership amidst educational transformations. A beacon for those seeking to foster environments where teachers and students thrive, this book is an essential tool for rekindling the passion and purpose at the heart of educational leadership.

> —Craig Aarons-Martin | Founder & CEO CCM Education Consulting Group

I strongly recommend Dr. Buskey's book, *A School Leader's Guide to Reclaiming Purpose*, not just to school administrators but to anyone searching for balance in their professional and personal lives. Frederick does an outstanding job combining current research with simple, practical, and proven strategies and techniques to help each reader identify and achieve their primary goals. Frederick has a unique ability to help readers find both hope and a plan for attaining personal and professional fulfillment!

> —Dr. Jan Osborn | Superintendent, Putnam County Educational Service Center

A School Leader's Guide to Reclaiming Purpose is an engaging handbook to help school leaders recalibrate and prioritize in order to rediscover the joy in their work. Effective leaders are purpose-driven and strategic employing high expectations to empower teacher and student growth. Perhaps one of the most important messages Buskey delivers is the notion that we must understand the difference between what is urgent and important in our daily tasks. With this understanding, we avoid the never-ending cycle of overwhelming tasks that do not allow us to engage in action that leads to impact.

> —Dr. Kim Winter | Dean, College of Education and Allied Professions, Western Carolina University

I am thrilled to recommend this captivating book that offers practical tools and a framework for navigating strategic leadership. This is EXACTLY what we need in today's climate! It identifies common challenges and provides useful, actionable solutions that will help you lead with purpose and clarity. Whether you're experienced or a rising leader, this book will undoubtedly leave you inspired and armed to excel!

> —Charle Peck, M.Ed., MSW | Keynote Speaker | Author | School Mental Health Consultant

Frederick Buskey hits the nail on the head with six stages of the leadership journey. This book is loaded with excellent tips, questions to ponder, and steps leaders of all experiences can benefit from to improve their practice and get focused on what matters in leadership. This book is a must for any leader looking to move out of the pull of urgency and into the realm of strategic leadership!

> —Darrin Peppard, EdD | Leadership coach, speaker, author, *Road to Awesome*, LLC

Dr. Buskey brings practicality back into leadership along with strategic and attuned thinking in regard to yourself and those you lead.

> —Alyson Perrin | Director of Elementary Education, Greenwood 50 School District,, South Carolina

A School Leader's Guide to Reclaiming Purpose by Dr. Frederick Buskey is a well-organized, or, as the reader will quickly realize, well-staged guide for school leaders. The practical and reflective strategies Dr. Buskey has incorporated throughout each chapter will help school leaders re-focus their energy on the most critical functions of school leadership as they navigate the intense social, political, and cultural challenges inherent in leading schools today. This book would be a useful tool for school leaders learning collaboratively in professional communities or as a self-paced guide for school leaders who don't have access to such communities but for whom this type of support is even more necessary.

—Dr. Hans Klar | Professor and Department Chair, Clemson University

I started working with Dr. Buskey many years ago, as a part of a leadership cohort, when I was a new elementary principal. As a new building leader, I can honestly tell you, I was super busy and the last thing I wanted to do was work with him. However, working with him was probably one of the best things I ever did for myself as a leader. Since that time, we have continued to stay in touch as professionals and friends. As I reflect on my experiences with Frederick, I can truly say that his approach to leadership development is the missing link, it helps leaders to not only understand but also prioritize, what's truly important in their role.

—Julian Gale | Director of Choice and Magnet Programs, Greenwood 50 School District, South Carolina

The tools and resources provided in this book provided our leadership team practical tools to effectively lead change in our school.

—Katie Joiner | Assistant Principal, School District of Newberry County, SC

I'm tired of teaching so I think I'll become a principal," said no one ever—at least no one I know ever said it out loud. Yet somehow in conversations over the years with teachers entering master's degree programs in educational leadership, assistant principals, and principals, this was often the reason which emerged.

On the other hand, we have five fingers. Many, I hope, chose to become educational leaders to lead. When someone asked me why I became a principal, I always said, "To save children and teachers before they drown." I had been a university professor in special education, and I saw so many teachers and administrators struggling every day when I visited schools. After many talks with those same people, I realized they were drowning because they didn't have the skills to do the work they were doing. Sure, they knew how to "teach." They knew how to "manage." Then why were they drowning? Because they didn't see themselves as leaders. Teachers are leaders! They lead somewhere between twenty and a hundred-and-twenty children or young people every day in how to learn. Principals are leaders! They lead teachers, students, parents, and staff every day—or at least they should. Leadership is about empowering others to do what they are in your building to do: learn, teach, support, lead. Frederick's book: A School Leader's Guide to Regaining Purpose will help you reexamine why you chose a leadership role. The six stages he defines, and helps you understand through examples, will truly guide you on a path of renewal for yourself. Not because someone said you needed renewal, but because we all do. This is your life. The hours you spend every day as teacher or administrator are the hours of your life. I hope you want to live your days in an environment where everyone is a learner and everyone is a leader—even if it's only specific to their own lives.

If you study the stages, explore the examples, and truthfully—for yourself—apply the strategies, you will experience the shift in the weight you often feel on your shoulders at the end of each day. I hope you will care enough about yourself and those you serve to read, study, and learn from this truly valuable information.

—Jacque Jacobs, PhD | Professor/Author

One of my most significant life lessons was that you do not have to make every mistake, you can learn from the mistakes of others, too. This is the book educational leaders need to learn from the mistakes of others. The advice within will get a new leader off to a great start or help recenter an experienced leader. It's like having your favorite education professor with you at all times, reminding you of all the important things you once knew but forgot when you got too busy! In challenging times, this book will connect you to how to do your job well and experience success for yourself, your staff, and your students.

—Dr. Leigh-Ann Alford-Keith | Senior Director of Innovative and Strategic Initiatives, Wake County Public School System, North Carolina

In this invaluable guide for K-12 school administrators, Dr. Frederick Buskey fully navigates the complexities of educational leadership, offering practical strategies to liberate leaders from the relentless demands of the urgent. With keen insights and actionable advice, this book empowers administrators to carve out precious time for the important work of supporting teachers and fostering a culture of strategic action in the pursuit of long-term success. A must-read for those seeking to transform their approach to leadership and prioritize what truly matters in the dynamic landscape of education.

—Robert Maddox | Superintendent, Lexington School District 4, South Carolina

If you're looking for an easy read that's also deeply researched, look no further than *A School Leader's Guide to Reclaiming Purpose* by Frederick Buskey. This engaging book examines how school administrators can effectively prioritize tasks and time through a hands-on accessible approach. Dr. Buskey has conducted extensive research on school leadership, synthesizing complex ideas into a format that is readily understandable. While insightful and informative, the book uses compelling examples, and research that bring the material to life and help school leaders identify what is crucial while also finding balance.

—Eleanor McCauley | Principal, Fairview School, Jackson County Schools, North Carolina

Dedication

This book is dedicated to the two most influential people in my life, without whom I could not have stayed true to my purpose, let alone written this book. To my mother, Barbara Buskey, who helped me believe I could write and to my wife and life partner Pam Buskey, who made sure I did write!

Table of Contents

Foreword

Let's face it. School leadership is hard. It involves a complexity of systems, people, politics, and pressures that result in a staggering number of highly qualified individuals dropping out of the profession. According to the National Center for Education Statistics, one in ten principals left the profession between the school years 2020-21 and 2021-22 (National Center for Education Statistics, 2023). Even though I began my education career long before then, I was almost one of those casualties.

As a former assistant principal and principal, I remember the overwhelming nature of the work. Like most education leaders, when I transitioned from the classroom to the office, I wanted to be the best version of an administrator for my students, teachers, and community. I devoted my early mornings to school preparation. I skipped lunch or ate on the run. I carried a notebook and wrote down every concern people brought to me so that I would not forget to follow up. I stayed up late after my wife and children went to bed so that I could answer emails and make to-do lists for the days ahead. I stopped exercising, eating healthy, spending quality time with my family, and I was burning out.

In my second year in administration, I almost gave up. One night my wife told me, "Will, the kids and I have accepted you are a husband and dad on the weekends only. The rest of the time, the school owns you." She went on to say, "In fact, you've become a shell of the man you used to be." That conversation prompted me to write a letter of resignation. I carried it to work, placed it in a folder, and set it on the corner of my desk. I told myself: I'm either going to find some more balance and perspective in taking care of myself and my family, or I'm handing in this letter and choosing another profession.

Thankfully, in the days and years ahead, I surrounded myself with other leaders for stronger accountability. I made new commitments to my own health and time with my family. There was no silver bullet in discovering more efficiency and productivity, but I began to discover some stronger practices, and I rediscovered joy in my work. As a result, seven years later in 2012, I was recognized as Oklahoma's Assistant Principal of the Year by my state principal association and the National Association of Secondary School Principals. Although that award was more a testament to the achievements of our students and teachers, I realized, looking back, that my recalibration played a big part in staying in the profession and seeing schoolwide improvements.

Oh, how I wish I had discovered sooner the ideas that you will discover in this generous book by Dr. Frederick Buskey. *A School Leader's Guide to Reclaiming Purpose* speaks to both the heart and the mind of leadership. In the pages ahead, you will find wise guidance and practical advice for avoiding the meltdown I was experiencing in my first years in school administration. Dr. Buskey's book is a field guide for school leadership. He skillfully explains the difference between urgent and important—a lesson when implemented as he instructs that will immediately save you time and energy. He also guides leaders through practices in prioritizing tasks and time, helps you understand how choices reflect your values, and unpacks the importance of practical takeaways like developing standard operating procedures.

Like a field guide helps a traveler or explorer find his or her way across new territory, this book will help you map out strategies for purpose-driven and people-driven practices. Along the way, you will discover step-by-step instructions and techniques to expand your capacity as a leader.

Are you ready to take action in the short term that will save you anxiety, mismanagement, and frustration in the long term? Hats off to Dr. Frederick Buskey for creating a survival guide like this for school leaders! Use the practices and advice in this book as your personal handbook. May it not only prevent more leaders from leaving the profession, but more importantly, may it provide you with space and permission to find joy and satisfaction in your work by expanding your capacity for helping students, supporting teachers, and reaching communities.

–William D. Parker

Founder of Principal Matters, LLC, and the host of *Principal Matters: The School Leader's Podcast*, with more than 1.3 million downloads to date. An Oklahoma educator since 1993, he is the author of three books, including *Pause. Breathe. Flourish.: Living Your Best Life as an Educator*

Reference: National Center for Education Statistics. (2023, July 31). Roughly One in Ten Public School Principals Left Profession in 2021-22 School Year. National Center for Education Statistics. https://nces.ed.gov/whatsnew/press_releases/7_31_2023.asp

Introduction

I remember the first time I met Mr. Jacks at his school. I had a scheduled appointment, but when I arrived, he was not in his office. His assistant Sheila said, "He's in the building somewhere. He's always on the move." She picked up a walkie-talkie to call him and then paused. Looking at me apologetically she said, "He didn't take his walkie with him today. That happens frequently."

Sheila and I proceeded to tour the building in hopes of finding the energetic principal and it wasn't long before we encountered him exiting a classroom. Mr. Jacks lit up and said, "Frederick, I'm so glad you are here! Come on, I want to show you some things!"

We invested the next hour touring the building, moving in and out of classrooms with Mr. Jacks providing context and history. His discussions always focused on teacher and student growth. He was a master at creating urgency with his teachers, and instilling in them the belief that their teaching had the power to transform students' lives. Accompanying his encouragement were high expectations for both teacher and student performance.

As I left the school, I thought about the contrast between Mr. Jacks and many other school leaders I knew. Most school leaders begin their journey with the goal of supporting and growing their teachers, but few take it to the level Mr. Jacks did. If Mr. Jacks was a rocket ship launched from Earth, he was somewhere out by Neptune, whereas many other well-intentioned, smart, hard-working school leaders don't make it past the moon.

The Journey

The school leader's journey is like a space mission in many ways. For 13 years I helped design, lead, and teach in school administration licensure programs at Western Carolina University and Clemson University. I got to know a lot of future administrators, and by virtue of consistently coordinating internships, I was able to observe, speak with, and learn from hundreds of practicing administrators. In them, I could see the different ways their own space missions were playing out.

Most of the school leaders I worked with began their journeys in a similar fashion. They imagined themselves traveling through the solar system of school leadership investing time in supporting and growing their teachers. They saw themselves observing in classrooms, providing transformative feedback, and empowering teachers to reach every student. I refer to this teacher-focused work as strategic leadership.

But so many of them barely made it out of Earth's atmosphere because they were hijacked by another force—the gravitational pull of urgency.

This pull is formed by the overwhelming number of urgent tasks confronting school leaders. These tasks suck them into a never-ending cycle of responding to what is most urgent. As they become stuck performing those tasks it feels almost impossible to carry out the actions which will help teachers have a substantive impact on student learning. The gravitational pull of urgency is just too strong.

Throughout this guide I'll use the analogy of a space journey. Specifically, I'll reference the remarkable journey of Apollo 13 which traveled to the moon and back from April 11-17, 1970. The ship was caught in the moon's gravitational pull due to an accident causing a massive loss of power.

The ship was unable to break away from the moon using its own power, so the crew, with guidance from mission control on Earth, executed a complex maneuver to wrap around the moon and use the moon's own gravitational pull to slingshot the ship out of the moon's atmosphere. Additional steps were taken to power down non-essential systems and redirect energy to only the most critical functions.

I've patterned the journey from urgent to strategic after Apollo 13's mission because the challenges and solutions carried out by the astronauts and their support team are in many ways similar to the challenges and solutions school leaders, with help from their support teams, must overcome to be able to be in the place where they can, like Mr. Jacks, invest large chunks of their time supporting and growing teachers.

Without this journey, many school leaders will remain trapped in orbit, forever trying to power their way away from the gravitational pull of urgency. This guide is the blueprint for escaping that pull, so you can reclaim your purpose for being a leader.

This guidebook takes you on a journey through six stages:

1. **Stage 1** is an examination of the gravitational pull of urgency with the goal of understanding what it is and why it is so hard to escape.
2. **Stage 2** is the U-turn, in which you begin to escape urgency by understanding the real problem keeping you trapped.
3. **Stage 3** is learning to power down by doing less of what is least important.
4. **Stage 4** is powering up, where you begin to implement important strategies to conserve and protect precious time, attention, and energy.
5. **Stage 5** is the slingshot which catapults you out of the gravitational pull by investing in being fully present with others.
6. **Stage 6** is the entry into strategic leadership by supporting and growing people.

Each stage consists of a core idea, frameworks, knowledge and skills to support implementation of the core idea, reflection questions, a challenge to apply your learning, and some closing questions. We'll get into how to make the best use of these components next.

Every Journey Needs a Guide

Moving from urgent leadership to strategic leadership doesn't happen all at once. It is a journey. As with many journeys, this one is easier with a guide. And, as with many people, we use guides differently.

I have written this book specifically to guide you from one stage to the next, but there are multiple ways to use this book. Your own learning style and context will determine what works best for you, but below I offer some options for how to get the most out of this guide.

Most adults learn by trying out new ideas, reflecting on the results, tweaking, reflecting, and finally adopting. This naturalistic style of learning taps into our innate ability to learn from our experiences and to adapt tools to our own needs. Taking this approach, you won't need to set a schedule for yourself. You will work at your own pace, investing more or less time on different stages as needed. You will likely complete the reflection questions and work through the challenge at each stage. In some stages you will pause and invest more time until you have mastered the content to your satisfaction. In other stages you may move through quickly, even skipping sections or challenges which don't seem necessary to you. The journey may take you three weeks or three months, depending on your needs and desires.

Another way to take this journey is as above, but adding someone to travel with. Two people, taking the journey together, retains the benefit of flexibility but adds an additional benefit of being able to process together, which can increase the rate and depth of learning.

Communication and collaboration are powerful forms of reflection, and having a partner also adds a layer of positive accountability.

You could also take a more structured approach by creating a schedule and providing yourself with specific intervals for completing each stage. Based on my experience and feedback from others, 3-4 weeks per stage is probably ideal. This provides time to read the content, reflect on it, try out the challenges, and then decide what changes to embrace and anchor into your practices. As with the naturalistic approach, you can do this more structured method with the benefit of another person.

My favorite approach to using this guide is as a book study for a group of district or building leaders. Focusing on one stage a month allows time to dig deeply into the practices and having a group adds a welcome layer of support and accountability. Additionally, a group of colleagues can better process and problem-solve, and even choose to adopt common practices, making reinforcement and sustainability more likely. If you want to use this guide as part of a book study, you can find supporting materials on my website at https://www.frederick-buskey.com/reclaimingpurpose.html

The final way I can envision using this guide is as a reference book. Using it this way, you might scan through the book, taking in the big ideas, and then diving more deeply into specific topics you were most interested in. Used this way, the book is more about helping you take different perspectives than reaching a specific destination. Alternatively, the book becomes a jumping-off point to go deeper into a specific concept that you deem important.

As I wrote this guide I imagined it as being an ideal tool for first-year assistant principals beginning their second semester, likely in January. The guide would then take them through the end of the school year. However, feedback from leaders at all levels leads me to believe the guide is not limited in utility by position, experience, or season. We are all subject to the tyranny of the urgent, regardless of our individual circumstances.

Preparing for the Journey

Each chapter of this book constitutes a stage in the leadership journey. Each stage follows a pattern designed to help you reflect, connect, and act. There are some things to *understand* and some things to *do* before beginning this journey.

What you need *to understand:*

- If you follow the steps of the book and complete the challenges, you will be a better leader. You will be investing more time in instructional leadership. I promise.
- I use conceptual frameworks. A conceptual framework organizes a complex concept and presents it in a simplified form. Conceptual frameworks are valuable because they make complex concepts more understandable and therefore more usable.
- I prefer simplicity, but it comes with a price. Conceptual frameworks vary in detail. Typically, the more detailed a framework, the more accurate it is in describing a concept. Frameworks with less detail are less accurate, but their simplicity makes them easier to understand and, more importantly, to use. Throughout this guide, I have prioritized simplicity over accuracy. In my experience it is much easier to act immediately on simple concepts, and immediate action is foundational to strategic leadership.
- Incremental change is more important than big change. Dramatic changes are usually the byproduct of a series of incremental steps and improvements. Growth will take place each day, little by little. You don't need to find **hours** a day to be an instructional leader. You need to use *minutes* strategically and

leverage them to their maximum benefit. This guide will take you there.

> You don't need to find *hours* a day to be an instructional leader. You need to use *minutes* strategically and leverage them to their maximum benefit.

- The stories in this guide are all based on real and specific events, but I have taken liberty to alter the originals in order to increase their teaching value. I have in some cases mixed multiple stories into a single parable, simplified or streamlined, and adjusted the context to create more clear and concise vignettes.

What you need *to do:*

Feel free to adapt the following suggestions to fit your unique person and context. The stages are designed to achieve a certain flow and rhythm. A stage is designed to span 3-4 weeks, but use whatever timing works best for you. A stage consists of the following content and actions:

- Beginning a stage:
  - Read, reflect, and write your response to *The Question. The Question* is the first thing you will encounter in each stage.
  - Read the content.
  - Respond to the reflection questions.
  - Review the challenges.
  - Check your schedule for the upcoming weeks.
  - Based on your schedule, identify the challenges you can realistically complete.

- Periodically throughout the stage:
  - Reflect on the previous days as they relate to your challenges.
  - Review your challenges and identify opportunities to work on them.
  - Set a clear intention to complete something small each day or week.
  - Mid-stage:
    - Check in with your accountability partner if you have one.
  - End of stage:
    - Use the Final Reflection prompts to reflect on your week.
    - Bonus: debrief with your accountability partner, a leader, or partner.

I hope you are committed to this journey. Let's begin.

STAGE 1

The Gravitational Pull of Urgency

The Question:

What prevents you from being more engaged in teacher development?

Goals for Stage 1: Trapped

1. *Reflect on the paradigm of Urgent Leadership below.*
2. *Differentiate between the four Quadrants of the Eisenhower Matrix.*
3. *Understand where you spend and invest most of your time.*

In a scene made famous by the movie *Apollo 13* (Broyles, et al., 1995), the team at NASA's mission control on Earth is figuring out how to get the crew home after an accident leaves their main ship severely damaged. Normally, the ship would use booster rockets to power out of the gravitational pull of the Moon's atmosphere. After the accident, however, the space capsule did not have enough fuel to break free of the Moon's gravity and make the return journey to Earth.

It is this problem, and the resulting solution, which inspired me to address the school leader's journey using the analogy of a space journey. To get the astronauts back on course for the return to Earth, the team had to find a way of operating which was fundamentally different from just powering through. They needed a different paradigm.

In April of 2018 I had an experience which inspired me to find a different paradigm. So much so that a year later I "pre-tired" from Clemson University and walked away from my work leading and teaching in Clemson's principal licensure program.

Since that experience, each time I visit a school, I ask administrators about their days, about getting into classrooms, and about their roles in teacher development. Not every story is the same, but there is a consistent theme. With some notable exceptions, the stories are similar whether it is a small school or a large one, rural or urban, elementary, middle, or high. The stories aren't always as dramatic as the story which follows, but the challenge is the same: it is hard to focus on supporting and growing people when you are caught in the gravitational pull of urgency.

> It is hard to focus on supporting and growing people when you are caught in the gravitational pull of urgency.

Five of Seven

I drive into the parking lot just after ten. I pull my sport coat from the back seat and shut the door, marveling at how warm and humid an April morning in South Carolina can be. As I walk towards the building, I reflect on what I know about this elementary school. It is typical of this rural region, a K-5 school with about five hundred students bused in from a large geographic area. I am here to check in on Tia, who is completing her administrative internship as part of her program at Clemson University, which I coordinate and teach in. I am also going to meet with Kelli, the school's assistant principal (AP).

After working with Tia, I am shown to Kelli's office. It is small, but comfortable, decorated with pictures of family and inspirational quotes.

Kelli sits behind her desk—her cheeks are flushed, her hair disheveled, and a disorganized layer of papers covers her desk. She holds a stack of yellow forms in her left hand and waves them at me as I take a seat opposite her.

"Kelli, what's wrong?"

Kelli shakes the papers in her hand.

"I have seven office referrals. It is ten o'clock in the morning. Each one will take me 30-45 minutes. My day is done! I won't get into classrooms, I won't be working with teachers, because I'm just going to do discipline all day long!"

Kelli looks close to tears. I know she aspires to be a principal. She is passionate about instructional leadership and wants to work with and grow her teachers. She knows what type of administrator she could be, but she feels her dream slipping away.

"Kelli, of those seven referrals, how many are more about the teachers' skills than the students' behaviors?"

There is a long pause as Kelli looks up into space and considers the question.

"Five. If the teachers had better relationships and classroom management strategies, five of these referrals would not exist."

I leave the office with a profound feeling of sadness. Here is a bright, experienced, and dedicated AP. She sees the needs and possibilities in her students and her teachers. She has read and worked to develop her instructional leadership skills, but she can't get out of her office long enough to put what she knows into practice.

I slide into the driver's seat of my car and sit. What bothers me most is this: She knows there are some teachers struggling with classroom *management. She knows if she could develop those teachers, she could stem the flow of referrals from those classrooms. And yet, she cannot find the time to work with those teachers. Something is desperately wrong here. And I know from working with some great school leaders that...*It doesn't have to be this way.

Kelli was caught in an "urgent" leadership model. The paradigm of urgent leadership is what keeps you trapped in the gravitational pull of urgency. The first step to escaping is to understand how it works and the impact it has on your leadership.

The Urgent Leadership Paradigm

Urgent Leaders:

- Focus on completing tasks.
- Deal with the most urgent tasks first.
- Treat symptoms as soon as they arise.
- Stay busy.

Urgent leaders are generally very productive. They bring a "can do" attitude and focus on getting things done. They are frequently well-organized and attempt to structure their days by focusing on tasks which need to get done. Barring unforeseen events, urgent leaders usually make good progress in the early parts of their day, but as issues arise, the to-do list gets replaced with a series of unplanned events we generically refer to as "fires."

Urgent leaders are flexible, so they adjust to the new demands quickly and step up to deal with new issues as they arise. Urgent leaders are quick to diagnose pain points, and their servant's heart guides them to ease the pains of others. Accordingly, they place a high priority on taking actions which improve situations and make the pain go away.

While urgent leaders are often highly productive, they frequently end their days frustrated and exhausted. They can find it difficult to get into classrooms or do other work related to teacher development and instructional leadership. Does this sound like you?

The very behaviors which make urgent leaders productive are the same behaviors which keep them trapped in a cycle of treating urgent issues all day long, day after day. It is a combination of mindset (what we think) and behaviors (what we do) which keep them trapped in the gravitational pull of urgency.

The gravitational pull is real. We live in a world where there is so much to do it can't all get done. Everyone wants more, and educators face louder demands from more stakeholders than ever before. Everyone wants something. Everyone needs something. And everyone is looking at you to take care of it!

Those demands are combined with a system of alerts and notifications which conspire to grab our attention with ever-increasing frequency. You are accessible through phone, text, email, and walkie-talkie. Your communication systems use red circles to alert you to new messages, supplemented by dings, pings, banners, and pop-ups.

> Everyone wants something. Everyone needs something. And everyone is looking at you to take care of it!

The plethora of communication modes leads people to expect instant and universal availability. "Did you get my email?" "Did you see my text?" "I left you a voice message."

It is not surprising that as we have made remote communication easier, more people are communicating more messages. But the nature of the communication is sabotaging your work. People ask for things because it is easy for them to ask. People share information because it is easy to share, regardless of its value or necessity.

The result is a never-ending cycle of tasks and interruptions. These combine with the urgent leader's natural tendencies to jump into action and get things done to create days filled with action but devoid of progress. You may prevent things from getting worse, but also fail to make things better.

The Eisenhower Matrix

1 Important Urgent	2 Important Not Urgent
3 Not Important Urgent	4 Not Important Not Urgent

The Eisenhower Matrix is a key tool in helping understand why urgent leadership is so unsatisfying. President of the United States, Dwight D. Eisenhower (1954, by The American Presidency Project), quoted a former college president as saying, "I have two kinds of problems, the urgent and the important." This quote was adjusted and led to the Eisenhower Matrix. The dichotomy was popularized by Stephen Covey (1989) in his book, the *Seven Habits of Highly Effective People*.

The Eisenhower Matrix consists of four Quadrants formed by the intersections of *urgent/not urgent* and *important/not important*.

Activities in Quadrant 1 must get done and must get done now. These are issues related to immediate safety and things with specific deadlines which are essential to the functioning of the school, as well as many legal and policy requirements. Quadrant 1 activities include being in IEP meetings, many duties related to test coordination, formal teacher evaluations, and supervision of students in specific situations (bus and car lines, etc.)

Activities in Quadrant 2 are important but lack the urgency of those in Quadrant 1. Much of the work of teacher development falls into Quadrant 2, as well as other proactive activities such as reflecting on and refining operations, developing standard operating procedures (SOPs), and building enduring community relationships.

Quadrant 3 activities are urgent, just as in Quadrant 1. Therein lies the problem. Quadrant 3 activities do not address the core responsibilities of schools—keeping people safe and improving student learning, yet they include a time-due component. Quadrant 3 tasks are urgent, but not important. Examples include things like scheduling special events, newsletters and other presentations, most email, and many aspects of compliance. Urgent leaders get into the habit of labeling all urgent tasks as "emergencies." There is a leaky water pipe–it is an emergency. A disgruntled parent is in the office–it is an emergency. The Assistant Superintendent is on the phone–it is an emergency. Or are these really emergencies? By virtue of being urgent, Quadrant 3 activities feel important, but are not truly important. We will dig into the differences between Quadrants 1 and 3 in Stage 2.

Quadrant 4 activities are neither urgent nor important. These activities provide no satisfaction and make no difference in the world, our schools, or our lives. Spending time in a workshop that doesn't apply to you is a waste of time. Writing a report nobody will read is a waste of time. Reading an article about how Sweden allows teachers to wear jeans every day is a waste of time.

In reality, many activities don't fit neatly into a single box. We will dig into the nuances in the next stage, but for now think of the four boxes this way:

1. Safety and critical operations
2. Teacher support and growth
3. All the stuff
4. Distractions which add no value

Soapbox

I don't discuss Quadrant 4 very often because I view it as largely irrelevant, but I think naming social media as a big Quadrant 4 activity is important.

I'm specifically talking about *personal* use of social media, not the things you do to promote your school or communicate with stakeholders. On the personal front, social media takes from you but provides little in return. Yes, you get to see what's happening with distant relatives or friends you haven't seen in years, but at what cost?

- Social media is designed to keep you engaged, so you usually spend far more time on it than you had intended.
- Social media subjects you to thousands of ads and media in tiny chunks which undermine your brain's ability to focus on and process complex information.
- Social media often leaves you feeling hollow, with a sense that while you may be connected, there is nothing meaningful in the connection.

If you want to do one thing to improve your leadership, get off social media. Pick up the phone and call a friend instead of scanning their posts. Or play with your dog. Either way, you'll be happier.

The Urgent Algorithm

You just explored the powerful combination of how your desire to serve others mixes with the availability and notifications in our modern communication systems. The situation is even more complicated.

When we work in Quadrant 1, we jump into action. When we resolve an urgent issue, we have a feeling of euphoria. This creates a cycle of charging into action, "fixing" something, and receiving a very satisfying feeling of accomplishment.

As you go through your days responding to urgent tasks, you become more and more addicted to the cycle, with the result being you prioritize what is urgent over what is important. Part of the power of the gravitational pull of urgency comes from the creation of these cycles, creating what some leaders refer to as "adrenaline junkies" and "dopamine devotees."

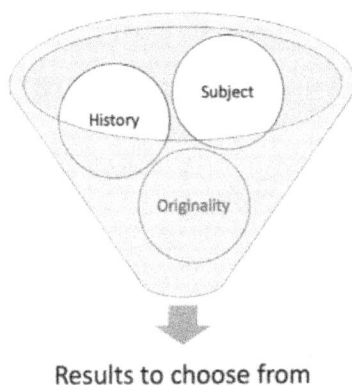

Results to choose from

This satisfaction cycle can be understood another way by understanding what happens when you conduct an internet search. You type in a topic and hit a button and your results pop up, but what's happening in the space between the click and the list of results? Your search engine is running an algorithm to get the "best" results. But what goes into the algorithm? What makes a list of results the "best"?

While Google's algorithms are cloaked in mystery, we do know they will take your topic, factor in your browsing history, and originality and recentness of content (The Verge, 2019). This produces a list which is unique to your search. It is not a definitive list, and it is not the best list; it is simply a list of possibilities arrived at through a series of calculations–the algorithm.

Like Google, our brains also work on algorithms which prioritize certain things. Typically, we consider symptoms, urgency, and history. This algorithmic thinking is good because it helps us respond quickly to issues in a predictable fashion. But when we are in the gravitational pull of urgency, we are largely unaware the algorithm is running, and because the algorithm is based on symptoms, urgency, and history, we are likely to continue responding to the same issues in the same ways, *regardless of their effectiveness.*

This is what was happening with Kelli. She received a discipline referral and the algorithm kicked in. She began processing the discipline referral immediately based on her prior experiences and the need to get it done. And as much as she was frustrated with the process, upon completing the referral, she undoubtedly felt a small sense of accomplishment. She had treated an issue, though she had not improved the situation.

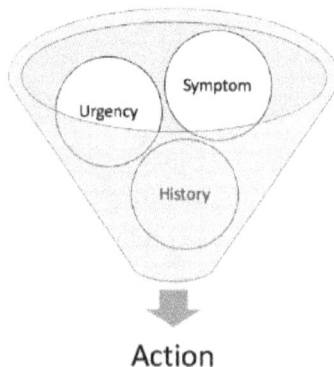

Action

I hope at this point you can see how urgency exerts its gravitational pull, and why it is so hard to escape. Time management and efficiency can help you get more done, but they will never help us escape the pull because *time is not the problem!*

Reflection

Kelli recognizes that her current way of operating isn't working. She knows powering through stacks of discipline referrals every day won't get her into classrooms. She's tried working harder and managing her time, but those strategies have not helped. She's desperate to try something else, but what?

Before moving onto the challenges, reflect on these questions:

1. Which elements of urgent leadership resonate with you?
2. In what ways are your days like those of an urgent leader?
3. In what ways are they different?
4. Think about other school leaders you know. To what degree do they exhibit the traits of urgent leadership?
5. Were there any ideas in this section you feel resistant to? Why?

Challenges: Challenges in this program are designed to be completed after reading the content for each stage. The big challenge is "required." The other challenges are optional. Please do not try to complete all of them. If you have the ability, complete one to three additional challenges. There are three indicators a given challenge might be good for you:

1. You want to do it. It may seem fun, or interesting, or make you feel accomplished.
2. You can immediately see it will benefit you.
3. You have an immediate negative reaction to doing it. Sometimes the things we least *want* to do are the things we most

need to do. That said, do not feel like you must embrace every challenge which triggers resistance.

The big challenge:

The big challenge for Stage 1 is to understand how you spend your time, what you accomplish, and what's left undone. This challenge involves tracking your time during the day. I suggest monitoring a solid week, though you can do more (or less) depending on your needs. Feel free to adapt this challenge to fit your needs.

Do the following:

- Create a "to-do" list for each day. Monitor what gets done and not done.
- Keep a running list of the unscheduled tasks which arise each day. There are a variety of ways to do this: running list, sticky notes, or an index card, recording everything in your physical or virtual calendar for example.
- When someone gives you a new task or comes to you with a task, record who it is, the task, and whether/how you engage in it.
- Keep all these records for the remainder of the journey. You will revisit them.

The intent of this activity is to help you begin to understand where your time goes while working, but many people choose to also track their time in their non-work hours and this can be very beneficial. If you are struggling with work-life balance, I encourage you to include your personal time in this activity.

Optional challenges:

- Identify an accountability partner and schedule a check-in every week or two. If you are taking this journey with another person or as part of a book study, scheduling regular times to touch base will be beneficial.
- Share publicly your intention to become a more strategic leader and ask people with whom you work or in your personal life to help hold you accountable. For example, you may share with a group of teachers that you are working to invest more time being an instructional leader and ask for their help in keeping you engaged in supporting them.
- Eliminate your personal use of social media for one day. This does not include professional usage to promote your school or what is required by your district. I encourage you to extend your social media hiatus beyond a single day and monitor your feelings closely.
- Work with other leaders to identify strategies for limiting interruptions while you are in classrooms or out of your office. For example, set phones so only specific people can reach you. Consider training front office staff on what constitutes an emergency. We will go into more depth on this in future stages.
- Schedule and attend a Friday afternoon debrief with your accountability partner.

1	2
Important **Urgent**	**Important** Not Urgent

3	4
Not Important **Urgent**	Not Important Not Urgent

Stage summary:

+ Urgent leaders focus on tasks.
+ Urgent leaders are driven by urgency.
+ Urgent leaders spend their time in Quadrants 1 and 3.
+ Urgent leaders spend much of their time reacting to events.

Final reflection:

The goal of this stage is to help you understand where and how your time is spent. Today's reflection will ask you to evaluate the tasks you completed in a variety of ways, so make sure to have all your records close by.

1. Work through your daily to-do lists and determine which quadrant each of the tasks was in. You may color code, number, or use some other way to visually divide the tasks. Here is some additional guidance to help you determine which quadrant a task belongs in:

    a. **Quadrant 1:** Safety issues which require immediate attention to avoid new or further harm. Legal or policy requirements with an impending deadline. Other things critical to operations.

    b. **Quadrant 2:** Most work related to supporting teachers and improving teacher quality. Time invested in understanding the needs of individual stakeholders (teachers, staff, parents, students) by being present with them and listening. Working on your own growth. All forms of self-care, including hobbies and time spent with people you care about.

    c. **Quadrant 3:** Tasks assigned to you by others which are not directly tied to safety, teacher development, or critical operations. Tasks which help other people do their jobs but aren't part of your job (more on this in the future). Tasks others could have done themselves. The line between Quadrants 1 and 3 is not clean, so do your best here. Your understanding of the Quadrants will grow throughout the journey.

    d. **Quadrant 4:** All personal social media.

2. Review your daily to-do tasks again and code them for whether they were completed.

3. Look for patterns. Don't be surprised if a larger percentage of Quadrant 2 items remain undone, even though many Quadrant 3 items are completed. Remember, this is a journey and how you use your time will change as you grow.

4. Examine the unscheduled tasks you spent time on. Identify the quadrant each one falls into. Are there any patterns?

5. Examine your list of tasks that did not appear on your to-do lists. Ask the following for each item:

    a. What quadrant was this in?

    b. Is this something you have dealt with multiple times?

    c. Is the same issue likely to occur again?

    d. Was it something only you could do? If not, who else could have done it?

    e. What did time spent on this specific task prevent you from doing?

    f. Was this task important to you?

Other questions:

1. Did you take any of the accountability challenges? If so, how did they go?
2. Were you able to step away from your personal social media? How did you feel?
3. Were you able to limit calls and interruptions when out of your office? How did you feel?
4. Did you notice yourself being more aware of the types of tasks you were doing?
5. Did you think about which quadrant various tasks were in as you planned or executed them throughout the week?
6. Did you detect any changes in your intentionality?

What's the Problem?

Earlier I asserted that time management and efficiency can help us get more done, but they will never help us escape the pull of urgency because

Time is not the problem!

For the rest of your weekend, sit with this question:

If time is not the problem, what is?

STAGE 2

The U-turn

The Question

If the approach you are using now (*Urgent Leadership*)
isn't taking you where you want to go, what
are some things you could change?

Goals for Stage 2: The U-turn

1. *Increase awareness of how you organize your work.*
2. *Shift your approach to tasks.*
3. *Reframe your priorities.*

In Stage 1 of the journey, we are caught in a gravitational pull. We can use time management and efficiency tools to try and escape, but they don't have enough power to provide a permanent escape and we inevitably get sucked back into the gravitational pull of urgency.

The solution the Apollo 13 team discovered was to use the power of the moon's own gravitational field to provide an initial boost to the lunar module by heading away from Earth and then using the Moon's gravitational pull to wrap around in a U-turn which would provide forward momentum. In the same way, by understanding the nature of the problem and adopting new perspectives, you are wrapping around the back side of the gravitational field and coming around in a U-turn to develop momentum for change. In this stage you will deconstruct the way you view your leadership and the work you do and then rebuild your perspectives.

One of the ways to make it easier to focus on priorities is to bring clarity to your own purpose as a school leader. As a school administrator, you have two responsibilities:

1. Keep everyone safe.
2. Improve opportunities for students to grow into adults who have agency in their lives.

From research and experience, we know the number one factor in student learning is the classroom teacher. So, we can reframe our priorities this way:

1. Keep everyone safe.
2. Support and grow teachers.

Distilling your leadership into two priorities may seem a bit simplistic, but think about this: if everyone is safe, and your teachers are doing great work with kids, how much easier does that make every other responsibility you have? If we can keep everyone safe, and support and grow our teachers, everything else is secondary.

The advantage of remaining simplistic is that it helps you stay focused on what is most important. I recognize that not everyone working through this journey is a principal or assistant principal. If you are in a different role, these two priorities may not ring true, but whatever and wherever you lead, there is a universal truth: improving the performance of the people you serve will improve your organization's ability to fulfill its purpose. Whether you are a district or county office leader, an instructional coach, or teacher, if you can support and grow the people around you, your school will become better at serving students.

Let's examine these two priorities through the lens of the Eisenhower Matrix. Keeping everyone safe constitutes much of the work of Quadrant 1, and Quadrant 2 is the quadrant of teacher support and growth.

Whatever and wherever you lead, there is a universal truth: improving the performance of the people you serve will improve your organization's ability to fulfill its purpose.

Support and Grow

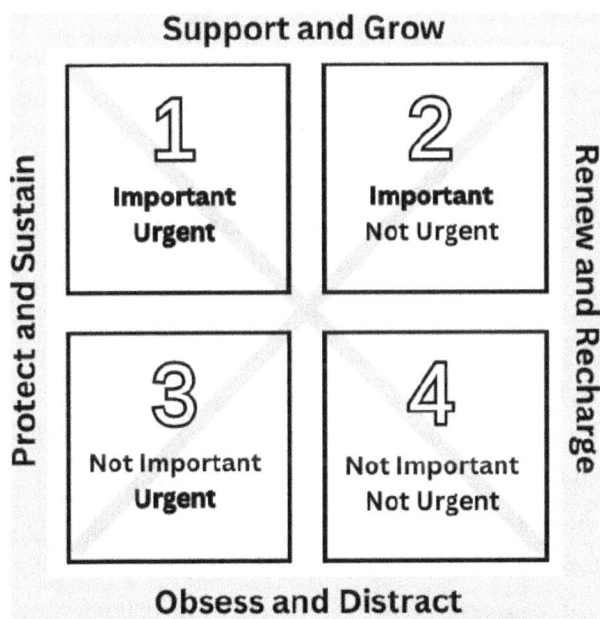

	Support and Grow	
	1 Important Urgent	**2** Important Not Urgent
Protect and Sustain	**3** Not Important Urgent	**4** Not Important Not Urgent	Renew and Recharge
	Obsess and Distract	

As noted previously, it is not that simple. Truthfully, there is no clear line between important and not important. There are many levels of importance, but for simplicity's sake we are going to assume three levels of importance:

1. The top two priorities: safety and teacher growth.
2. Other things important to the smooth operation of the school and to fulfilling community and legal expectations and requirements.
3. A bunch of other stuff which does not have a significant impact on any of the above.

We can visualize these levels of importance as overlapping the four quadrants:

+ Supporting and growing others overlaps Quadrants 1 and 2.
+ Protecting and sustaining the organization overlaps Quadrants 1 and 3.
+ Renewing and recharging oneself overlaps Quadrants 2 and 4.
+ Obsessing and distracting overlaps Quadrants 3 and 4.

Another important thing to keep in mind is that *urgency has as much to do with feeling* as it does with an actual deadline. Many tasks *feel* urgent, even when they don't have deadlines at all.

The Eisenhower Matrix visually shows us the problem with Urgent Leadership. Urgent leaders are driven by Quadrants 1 and 3. Urgent leaders look for time management and productivity strategies to help them get things done, *but time management is not the problem!*

The real problem is reflected in putting Quadrant 3 work in front of Quadrant 2 work. If you begin focusing on supporting and developing teachers instead of completing the urgent tasks in Quadrant 3, you will begin addressing the real problem. The real problem is priority management.

The real problem is priority management.

By shifting the priorities in your day, from urgent to important, you can fundamentally change the nature of your work. So then, how do you move from managing time to managing priorities?

The Six Dimensions of Organization

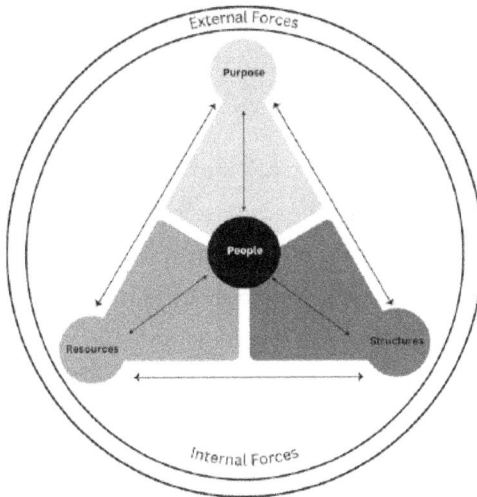

The Six Dimensions of Organizations is a conceptual framework for understanding how to improve organizational outcomes by focusing on organizational alignment. Like any conceptual framework, it is a simplistic representation of a complex phenomenon.

All organizations share four basic components: people, purpose, structures, and resources. In addition to the four basic components, external and internal forces make up the final two dimensions.

Each of these dimensions can work with or against the others. When any component is out of alignment with the others, friction is created. Friction inhibits organizational functioning and success. In a perfect organization, all elements are aligned. In the real world, every organization is misaligned in some way. In high-performing organizations, the degree of misalignment is small. In struggling organizations, the degree of misalignment is high.

People

People's attributes:

- Knowledge
- Skills
- Dispositions
- Health

People are the individuals who work and live within or are connected to the school. Students and families are our reason for existing, but for the purposes of this guide, we are focused on staff, and most particularly on teachers. Better teachers equal a better school.

The uniqueness of each individual within the organization can enrich the organization, but they can also contribute to misalignment. People have agency and lives outside the organization. This combination of factors usually means people have their own purposes (yes, multiple) which may or may not align to those of the organization.

People have unique attributes which include knowledge, skills, dispositions, and health. When we talk about growing teachers, we are talking about nurturing and improving these four attributes.

Knowledge is what people know. What they know about teaching, about students, about themselves, about leadership…about everything. Knowledge can be built on and leveraged. We can also consider

> People have unique attributes which include knowledge, skills, dispositions, and health. When we talk about growing teachers, we are talking about nurturing and improving these four attributes.

what teachers don't know, because that can be as impactful as what they do know.

Skill is the ability of teachers to apply what they know, although skills do not reflect an exact correspondence with knowledge. A teacher may not be able to manage a classroom even though they know the components of good classroom procedures. For example, teachers may create safe and supportive classrooms which meet the needs of diverse learners even if they don't have training in diversity, equity, or inclusion.

Dispositions are attitudes and beliefs. They constitute how a person views their world, how they interpret the actions of others and the conditions of their environment. Dispositions have a strong influence on how knowledge and skills are used. A teacher who had been treated poorly by a previous administrator may have a negative disposition towards all administrators. A teacher caring for a terminally ill parent may prioritize supporting their parent over preparing for lessons. A teacher who believes they can make a difference with each student is likely to work to expand their knowledge and convert knowledge into skills.

Most importantly, people have *health*. This includes physical as well as social and emotional health. Health, in all its forms, influences the work people can do and, of course, the quality of their lives. As people become healthier, their capacity to grow and to act on their knowledge and skills expands. In my experience it also seems to be true that when we grow in knowledge and skill, our health is positively impacted.

Purpose

Purpose is complex because in every organization there are multiple purposes at work. There is value in beginning with why, as Simon Sinek (2011) encourages us to do, but the question then becomes "Which why?" or "Whose why?"

Leaders and organizational theorists often act as if each organization has a singular purpose, usually something articulated in the mission statement. For example, a high school mission statement might include something about preparing global citizens who, as adults, have agency over their lives. However, organizational purposes are much more complicated than the words in a mission statement. Purposes can be official, but they can also be unofficial. Not all purposes are stated, and not all purposes are shared collectively.

In contrast to a single clear purpose, there are actually multiple purposes at work in every school—some sanctioned, some not; some written, some not; some shared, and some not. Let's look at some examples.

In addition to the mission statement, most schools also have other official purposes, such as increasing test scores or placing x% of their students into four-year colleges. Each of these official purposes is probably written into a strategic plan or some document that makes it easy for people to see and these goals are collective in that they are widely supported among the members of the school.

Some official purposes may be unstated; for example, a desire to have an image of being on the leading edge of innovation. Such a goal may be understood and embraced by the collective, but not be written down anywhere.

Finally, different people may bring different purposes which will impact the other dimensions of the organization. In a certain sense, every adult brings their own purpose to school, and these multiple purposes influence what we do.

Purpose:
- Official/Unofficial
- Stated/Unstated
- Collective/Individual

Consider this scenario:

Imagine I'm the new principal of an elementary school. I work in a rural environment where it's typical for elementary principals to get promoted to middle school, and middle school principals to get promoted to high school. I really want to be the high school principal.

My purpose is to get myself promoted to the middle school as fast as I can. It may not drive everything I do, but it will influence some of my decisions. I might be oversensitive to how my actions are viewed by the superintendent or to district office expectations. This is not necessarily a bad thing, but if there's a decision to make and maybe decision A is better for my elementary school, but Decision B looks better at the district office, I may choose B because I have an alternative purpose.

People Before Purpose: My original model of the Six Dimensions prioritized purpose, with people, structures, and resources supporting the purpose. Emphasizing a "purpose-driven" organization is consistent with most of the literature on organizational improvement. Open any leadership text and you will be inundated with words like vision, mission, goals, and objectives. So, what made me move from a purpose-driven to a people-driven view?

There are four primary reasons. First, people are the purpose. We entered education to impact kids and, after leaving the classroom, the best way to impact kids is to support and grow teachers. In doing so, we create better outcomes for students, a better place to work for teachers and staff, and we fulfill our most important purpose.

The second reason for putting people first is the lack of clarity of school purpose. As noted previously, there are many different purposes at work in a school. When we try to align people, structures and resources, which purpose should we be aligning them to? Do we embrace a curriculum and teaching methods to prioritize developing student agency? Or do we prioritize materials and programs that raise test scores?

The different purposes within schools can conflict, especially when we conflate measures (test scores) with missions (student agency), which is inescapable given the legal, political, and fiscal entrenchment of a numbers-driven educational system.

Thirdly, leaders have power over others, and therefore have an ethical obligation to care for those they wield power over. This is certainly true for hierarchical leaders wielding legitimate power, but it is also true for non-hierarchical leaders wielding "softer" forms of power. If I am willing to lead you, I must put your health and well-being at the forefront of my concerns.

Finally, focusing on people facilitates the work of growing and supporting teachers. When we put people first, we prioritize their growth, resulting in better people, and in schools better people equals better teachers, and better teachers equals better schools.

When we put people at the center of our leadership, our decisions become clearer. In Stage 6 I'll talk about building a system to support continual teacher growth, but without a strong system, think about how you decide where to focus improvement efforts. Is it based on which test scores you are trying to raise? Or maybe whatever the district leadership is calling for? Or maybe the hot new program sweeping the education world?

If we take a person-centered approach, the needs become clearer. When we put people first, we learn about those people. We learn about their strengths and how to leverage them. We learn about their desires, and how to help fulfill them. We learn about their barriers, and how to support them. This person-centered approach helps us support and grow teachers more effectively than any stock program, and better teachers equal better schools.

And then there is this…

On Halloween Eve in 2020, my wife Pam lost her mother, Margaret. Six weeks later her oldest brother Scott passed away at the age of 57. The previous two years had been a grueling, heart-wrenching march to the end for both Margaret and Scott. Pam was exhausted, emotionally and physically spent. On top of trying to cope with a huge hole in her life, she was, like the rest of us, trying to navigate the COVID pandemic. And yet, she went to work every day, taught her students, graded assignments, and served on committees. She showed up—but only partially. Only the part she could still bring forward. The rest of her was occupied, trying to make sense of and adapt to a sick world, one without her mother and brother.

During this time, I stood inside my wife's personal life, and I watched her muddle through her outside work life. It was obvious that she wasn't as good a teacher or colleague that semester. She wasn't as good at fulfilling the school's mission. But none of that mattered. What mattered was her, and the road to healing. A purpose-driven leader would view poor performance as a problem. A people-driven leader would see that same performance as part of the human journey and would focus on helping her make that journey in the best way possible.

During this period of mourning, Pam's student evaluations were lower, and if she had been teaching a tested area in k-12, her students would surely have scored lower on the state assessment. This leads me to the final reason for putting people before purpose.

From my perspective we have convoluted and confused the purpose of education. In our obsession to quantify student progress we have elevated things that can be easily measured, like facts and formulas, above things which are harder to measure such as agency, resiliency, and collaboration. We now make decisions based on numerical calculations instead of human ones. In a particular school, one reading intervention teacher is able to work with 20 students, but 50 students are reading below grade level. Which 20 students receive services? Do you focus on "bubble kids"—the students whose test scores are just below passing–in order to raise test scores? There are many criteria we could use to make the decision about who *does not* receive services, but basing it solely on who can give the school a bump on paper does not seem appropriate. Maybe you have made a similar choice? You can say that I don't understand the pressure or the expectations–but that is exactly my point. The purpose has become distorted.

It seems to me that a more just way to structure our organizations is around the health and capacity of the people within the school. It is a way to escape the tyranny of numbers and a way to increase the meaning and power of our work as leaders. An associate superintendent told me escaping the tyranny of numbers was not possible. I hear that, and the amount of policy, accountability, and funding tied to the numbers is evidence that my friend is correct. So I acquiesce; we cannot escape the tyranny of the numbers. But we can choose how we approach our work as leaders. Raising test scores and creating better teachers are not the same thing. That said, supporting and growing teachers will almost always lead to better scores. You can begin with the numbers, or you can begin with the people. The beauty is, you get to choose.

Structures

Structures exist in three different forms:

- *Physical structures* include buildings, as well as the shape and arrangement of the rooms and furniture in those buildings. Physical structures play a critical role in shaping how people work, especially regarding community and hierarchy. Physical structures can promote or inhibit collaboration, increase or decrease isolation, and flatten or exaggerate hierarchy.
- *Legible or codified structures* are the written policies, procedures, and legal requirements which influence and shape our work. I refer to them as legible because they are written and visible.

- *Intangible structures* are the expectations, rituals, and routines which are not formally codified but nonetheless exist. They exist in verbal form. They exist in the stories we tell, the praise we give, the expectations we hold, and the rituals we observe.

All these structures shape and give form to how we do our work. When these structures are closely aligned to the purpose of the school, they make it easier for the people to work towards achieving the purpose of the school. If the structures are misaligned to the purpose, then the structures make it harder for people to do the work to fulfill the school's purpose.

Structures have a strong influence on people, in both subtle and obvious ways. Structures can make it easier for people to use their knowledge and skills, or structures can impose barriers.

A tangible example of how structures influence school environments can be seen in how the remnants of industrial schooling practices create barriers to our modern expectations for teaching and learning. Expectations for students to be college ready and to be independent and creative thinkers requires different ways of teaching, but the physical structures and to a large extent the codified structures haven't substantively changed over the past one hundred years. In many places, the purpose of school is fundamentally at odds with the structures and the policies in place.

Resources

Resources come in two different forms: Dynamic and static. Dynamic resources can change over time. Dynamic resources include money and tangibles. Money is the amount of purchasing power an organization has. Tangibles are the physical and digital possessions such as furniture, buses, books, and computers.

The amount of money a school has access to changes over time. For example, by passing a local sales tax or having the state cut education spending. The amount and type of tangibles we have also changes over time based on what we purchase and what breaks, gets used, or becomes obsolete. For example, most schools have many more computers and technological tools now than they did pre-pandemic.

A case may also be made to include people's knowledge and skills as dynamic resources. For simplicity's sake I have chosen to keep knowledge and skills in the people dimension, but it is appropriate to think of them as dynamic assets that can grow, or shrink, over time. In contrast, static resources do not change. The two critical static resources are time and attention.

Time: Time refers to each individual's time, collective time, and organizational time. Individual time is the amount of available time for work any individual has, for example forty hours per week. Collective time refers to the total amount of time available for a given group of people. For example, a team of five people may have a collective amount of two hundred hours. Organizational time is measured by days, weeks, months, and years. Organizational time refers to the length of time defined by deadlines or other landmarks. For example, the launch date for a new initiative may be three months away, so the organization has three months of temporal resources to prepare for the launch.

Every individual only has twenty-four hours in a day. No matter how well we organize it, no matter how productive we are, no matter what kinds of time-saving tips we can put into effect, the actual amount of time available to us and to every person working in the school is capped. There is little we can do to increase the amount of time available to us as individuals or to the school as a whole.

Attention: The second static resource is attention. As human beings, we can only attend to a limited amount during each moment. We can bring our entire attention to one task, or we can multitask by splitting our attention between more than one thing. However, we have not increased the amount of attention, we have simply reallocated it. A big challenge is that Quadrant 2 work is generally complex and requires a higher degree of attention, making multitasking difficult, ineffective, and even counterproductive.

> Quadrant 2 work is generally complex and requires a higher degree of attention, making multitasking difficult, ineffective, and even counterproductive.

How much can we attend to at one time?

Imagine you are a classroom teacher and after an observation the instructional coach leaves you with an "I wonder..." statement. "*I wonder if you had a problem on the board for the students when they entered the classroom if you could get class started faster.*"

A day later the assistant principal does a walk-through of your classroom and leaves another "I wonder..." statement. "*I wonder if you did more group work if kids would be more engaged in class.*"

Another day passes and the principal observes and offers feedback. "*I wonder if you asked higher order thinking questions if your students would learn more.*"

Three people have come into your classroom and made three suggestions.

+ Which one should you attend to?
+ How do you initiate changes to classroom procedures, higher order thinking, and grouping students at the same time?
+ And if you are a first-year teacher, all your attention may be consumed just figuring out what you are supposed to be teaching the next day.

Attention is a finite and critical resource we often overlook.

Attending to one thing means we can't attend to something else.

Anytime we make a demand, put out a new initiative, or ask people to engage in a specific practice, we are consuming their time and attention. Whether it's a teaching practice, something regarding policy, or anything else, every task comes with a cost of time and a cost of attention.

Because we have limited time and attention, everything we do in a school, every demand we place on a teacher or an administrator comes with an opportunity cost. The opportunity cost is the time and the attention we could have spent or invested on something else. The key question when considering new initiatives and making changes is not, "Can we do this?" The key question is, "Is there a better way to invest our time and attention?"

> The key question when considering new initiatives and making changes is not, "Can we do this?" The key question is, "Is there a better way to invest our time and attention?"

External Forces

External forces are largely beyond the control of the organization, but they impact the organization in substantive ways. External forces come in three forms:

- **Legislation and governance** create rules, laws, and policies which impact the organization. For example, federal and state governments have created laws and policies which require schools to give normed tests and, in many cases, include sanctions and rewards based on test performance. The large-scale implementation of testing regimes impacts every element of the school.

- **Social and political forces** largely involve discourse around and at schools and impact how people outside and inside the school view the organization. These forces often influence governance as seen in the current efforts to censor books and curriculum based on specific political agendas and ideologies.
- **Naturally occurring events** include extreme weather and, of course, pandemics. Less dramatic examples include the changing of seasons.

Internal Forces

We can think of internal forces as culture. This is simplistic but useful. Internal forces are shaped by how the purpose, structures, and resources impact the people within the school.

When purpose, structures, and resources are aligned to people's knowledge, skills, dispositions and health, internal forces will be smooth and positive. In an aligned school, people have the resources they need, and the structures make it easier for them to work towards a powerful purpose. People find their work rewarding and less stressful and they will be able to have the maximum positive impact.

In contrast, misalignment creates stress and inhibits performance. In misaligned schools, rules and expectations (structures) run counter to the purpose, people are under-resourced or experience too many demands on their time and attention, and they become stressed and frustrated, resulting in a negative culture.

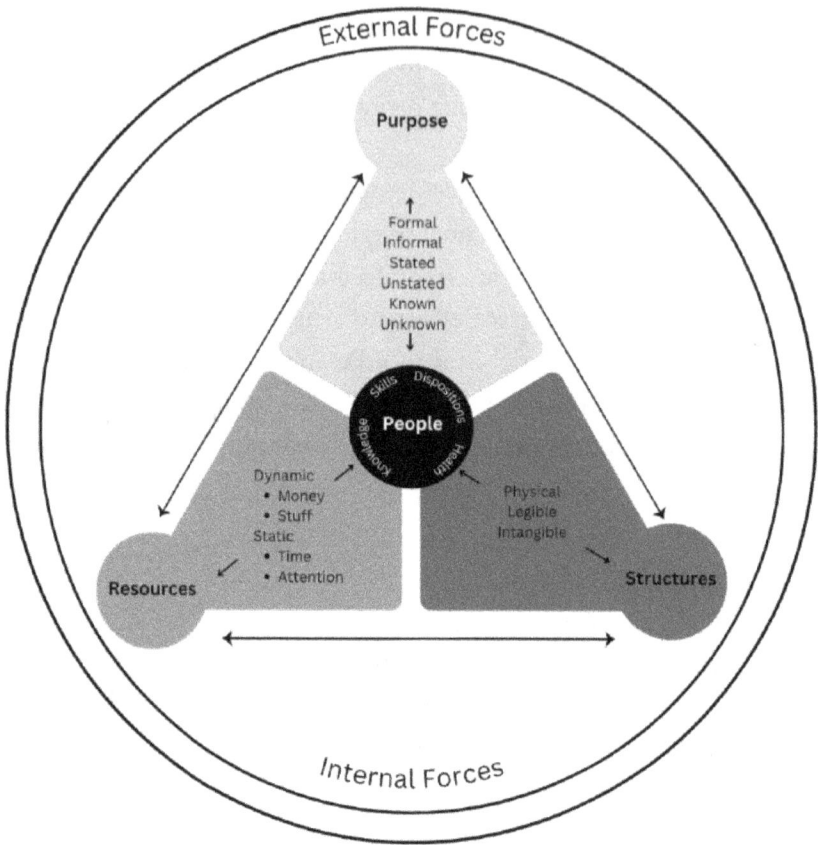

The Problem of Alignment

Misalignment is unavoidable in all but the simplest organizations, and schools are very complex places. The value of viewing organizations through an alignment lens is that there really is only ever one problem: Something is not aligned. The misalignment will always revolve around people and there are only four basic permutations:

1. The purpose is unclear or there are multiple conflicting purposes which distract and confuse people.

2. People do not have the resources they need to do the work they aspire to.
3. The structures present barriers to people's work and health.
4. People lack the knowledge, skills, dispositions, and/or health to do the work.

For example, imagine a scenario in which a school has adopted professional learning communities (PLCs), but the practice is having little to no impact on the quality of teaching. Why? Something is out of alignment.

Perhaps the reason for meeting in PLC teams is unclear. Are the PLCs about teaming? Or data analysis? Or for learning specific skills? Alternatively, perhaps teachers view the emphasis on "data-based decisions" to be at odds with their own priorities of nurturing students. In either of these cases, the outcome may be teachers who are confused and, as a result, do not prioritize PLC work.

The lack of PLC impact could also be a resource issue. If the PLC emphasizes skill acquisition, but teachers are already being asked to grow skills through other training and programs, they may not be able to attend to growing in multiple areas at once—they simply do not have the time and attention to devote to it all.

The PLC implementation may have been flawed. If there is not a clear and structured agenda, time might be wasted. If protocols aren't being used with fidelity, the process may not work. Or maybe the meetings are too few and far between. These are all structural issues which, because of the way we have implemented the PLCs, contributes to their ineffectiveness.

Finally, the teachers may not have the skills, knowledge, dispositions, or health to capitalize on the PLC opportunities. Teachers might be overwhelmed by classroom management issues. A new teacher may still be learning the curriculum and not have the foundational knowledge to adopt more advanced teaching strategies. A teacher may have decided that "nothing will work" because the students "don't care."

These are all examples of misalignment. If we want more effective PLCs, we need to figure out what the source of the misalignment is. Using the six dimensions as a reference point makes the process simpler.

> Supporting = Increasing alignment
>
> Growing = strengthening knowledge, skills, dispositions, and health

When we look at organizations through an alignment lens, the work of leadership becomes clear. When we talk about supporting teachers, we are talking about increasing organizational alignment. When we talk about growing teachers, we are talking about increasing or improving their knowledge, skills, dispositions, and health.

In this stage we have identified the two key responsibilities of school leaders:

1. Keep everyone safe.
2. Support and grow teachers.

We have reframed the challenge of our work, focusing on priority management rather than time management. We have determined the role of leadership is to align the four dimensions for the school to create a positive culture that facilitates people's growth, life, and work. We have an expectation for school leaders to make changes, but we need to be crystal clear about the purpose of any change we make. The purpose of leadership is to keep people safe and support and grow teachers. The responsibility of leadership is to use change processes to create strong organizational alignment.

I hope at this point you are beginning to view your work differently.

There is one more piece of the puzzle needed to complete the U-turn: choice.

> The purpose of leadership is to keep people safe and support and grow teachers. The responsibility of leadership is to use change processes to create strong organizational alignment.

The Three Epiphanies

Several years ago, I had a conversation which changed the way I thought about my work and which led to much of what I'm sharing here. I was working with the principal of a small elementary school with about 250 students. She had no assistant principal, so everything fell on her. I asked her about the hours she worked. She responded she typically left her building around 4:00, working between 8-9 hours a day.

I was astounded. Many principals I talk with work long hours. Some of them consistently work twelve-hour days. I asked how she got everything done. She said, "Oh, I can never get everything done, but what doesn't get done will be there tomorrow."

Over the next few weeks, I continued to reflect on our discussion. Slowly, my understanding deepened, and finally, one day, I understood. There were three powerful truths underlying the way the principal viewed her work, which I now refer to as The Three Epiphanies:

Epiphany 1: There is Not Enough Time

This is the easiest of the epiphanies to embrace. There are unlimited needs in a school. Even if you had none of the urgent tasks to do, you could fill your entire day helping teachers to grow and still have things left undone. It is the nature of the work.

Epiphany 2: I Choose Where to Invest My Time

If you accept you can't do it all, then you need to make choices about what does and doesn't get done. When you choose to spend the first few minutes of the school day taking care of email (Quadrant 3), it also means you are *choosing* to not invest time with your teachers and students by connecting and helping them get their days off to great starts.

Here's the wonderful thing about accepting it can't all get done: *You* choose what gets done and what doesn't. *It may not feel like you have choices* because you have been unintentional about making them. You have let the gravitational pull of urgency guide the direction of your work. However, the key to escaping this pull is to embrace the idea that you do make choices. You can *choose* to run on autopilot from urgent task to urgent task, or you can *choose* to make purposeful decisions. This brings us to the third epiphany.

Epiphany 3: My Choices Reflect My Values

For me, this has been the most challenging of the three epiphanies. It is scary because it forces me to confront some inconsistencies between my beliefs and my actions.

When you choose to spend forty-five minutes updating a "Student of the Week" bulletin board, instead of investing time observing and post-conferencing with a teacher, you are putting your desire to celebrate students ahead of helping a teacher get better.

When you choose to do one thing, you are also choosing to not do something else, because you can't do it all. Until now, the biggest influencer in your decisions may have been urgency. What the three epiphanies can help you understand is that you can choose to prioritize importance over urgency.

Reflection

Remember Kelli, the assistant principal struggling with discipline? Let's look at her situation through this different lens. An urgent leadership mindset led her to focus on tasks related to discipline. She knew there were teachers who needed her support, but the "urgent" things were the referrals and other tasks that kept demanding her time and attention. This perpetuated the cycle of treating the symptoms (referrals) ensuring that the cycle will repeat on a regular, if not daily, basis.

Now Kelli realizes the problem isn't time; it is priorities. She sees that when she chooses to leap into action over each urgent thing hitting her desk, she is also choosing to not support one of those struggling teachers. She believes teachers are critical to the success of the school, but now she's realizing her priorities have not been consistent with that belief. Now, Kelli is beginning to pay attention to the choices she is making and thinking about how she can make different choices.

Each of the questions below is designed to help you reflect on one or more of the key concepts from this stage:

1. The first step in this stage was to reframe the role of school leadership as having two dominant responsibilities: keep everyone safe and support and grow teachers.
   a. Is it that simple? Why or why not?
   b. If you could help teachers increase their abilities by 50%, what kind of impact would this have on your students?
   c. If you could spend fifty minutes a day totally focused on teacher development, what impact would this have on teacher quality?
   d. What impact would this work have on you?
2. If the work of leadership is about creating alignment, what implications does this have for your choices?

3. Do your challenges look differently when viewed through an alignment lens?

4. Some people can find the three epiphanies daunting. If you have freedom to choose, you increase your accountability for choosing wisely. If your values reflect your choices, you must confront what you value.

    a. Which of the epiphanies challenges you the most?

    b. If the three epiphanies have created a sense of dissonance, what can you do to resolve it?

    c. Do your choices reflect your values?

Challenges: Remember the big challenge is required. The other challenges are optional. Do what makes sense given your time, interest, and capacity.

The big challenge:

The big challenge this week has two distinct parts:

1. Continue to create a daily task list but make the following changes:

    • Organize the list into quadrants by quartering the page to mirror the Eisenhower Matrix.

    • Write your tasks into the appropriate quadrants. Be ruthless in separating Q1 from Q3!

    • You MUST include a minimum of two items in Quadrant 2 which focus on supporting and growing teachers. These may include a form of classroom observation or coaching conversation. They may also include having simple conversations which help you learn more about the teacher such as asking them to reflect on a lesson or something else. Focus on watching, asking, and listening. Please avoid telling and talking. This list may not include mandatory observations or conferences—those are Q1.

+ Try and begin each day by engaging in a Q2 task.

2. When presented with a new task to do, ask three questions:
   + What quadrant is this task in?
   + Does this deal with a structure, resource, person, purpose, or a combination?
   + Do I choose to do this task? You always have a choice. Recognize it and own it.

Optional challenges:

1. Review your notes from last week and recode them as being a safety focus, teacher development focus, policy requirement, or other. What do you notice?
2. Ask one or more teachers to talk about the demands on their time and attention. You may ask this question in general terms, or you may ask more specifically about the demands of a specific initiative or responsibility. Just listen. Provide no feedback. This counts as a Q2 activity for purposes of the big challenge.
3. Reflect on the different issues or challenges you spend your time dealing with. Evaluate each of them through the lens of the Six Dimensions. What forms of misalignment do you see? What would need to change to bring about greater alignment?
4. Reflect on a major initiative being implemented in your school:
   a. From an alignment perspective, what problem is it trying to solve?
   b. How much time and attention does it require?
   c. Are the current school structures aligned to the demands of the initiative?
   d. Are the various changes being made by the initiative increasing school alignment?

5. Ask one or more teachers what would be one change which would make their job easier. Choose a teacher who has a positive disposition towards students. Do not respond to the answer, just be quiet and listen. If you want more details just say, "Can you say more?" Then be quiet. After the discussion, think about the issue of alignment. This counts as a Q2 activity.

6. Schedule and attend a Friday afternoon debrief with your accountability partner.

I can't do everything.

I choose what get's done and what doesn't.

My choices reflect my values.

Stage summary:

+ There are six dimensions to organizations: people, purpose, structures, resources, internal forces, and external forces.
+ Putting people before purpose helps us focus on improving schools by growing teachers.
+ The work of leadership is to bring schools into alignment to make high quality teaching easier.
+ The three epiphanies help us to clarify our decisions:
  ◦ There is not enough time to do everything.
  ◦ We choose what gets done (and not done).
  ◦ Our choices reflect our values.
+ When we stop trying to manage time and begin managing priorities, we turn ourselves in the direction to escape the gravitational pull of urgency.

Final reflection:

The goal of this stage is to help you change how you look at your work and, in turn, reshape how you identify priorities. There is a lot to dissect in this stage and having someone to work through it with you can be very helpful. I encourage you to complete this reflection with an accountability partner or with your team or community.

1. Where are the lines between the quadrants clear and easy to see?
2. What kinds of tasks are difficult to distinguish between quadrants?
3. If someone above you requires you to do something, but that something is not important (example: count all the pencils in the building), what quadrant does it belong in? Why?

4. Are you looking at tasks differently? If so, how have your thoughts changed?
5. Are you looking at supporting and growing people differently? If so, how have your thoughts changed?

Moving out of *Urgent Leadership* requires a shift in perspective, which we have begun tackling in this stage. It also requires a shift in behavior and the creation of systems. As you have doubtless experienced already, you cannot ignore something just because it is in Quadrant 3. It still needs to be accounted for. In Stage 3, we look at some strategies designed to account for Quadrant 3 activities without doing them yourself.

Powering Down

Goals for Stage 3: Powering Down

1. *Learn to filter requests for your time.*
2. *Develop strategies for giving people back their monkeys.*
3. *Identify opportunities to leverage the skill of people around you.*

As Apollo 13 began to wrap around the moon, it also had to conserve energy by powering down all non-essential systems. Powering down allowed the astronauts to then redirect power to the systems which were most important. Stages three and four work closely together. In Stage 3, we are powering down by learning how to avoid tasks, and by reconditioning other people's expectations of us. In Stage 4, we'll redirect that power to more productive systems.

Just because a task is now labeled as Quadrant 3 doesn't mean it will take care of itself. While you should be doing as little as possible in Quadrant 3, the organizational structures which funnel those tasks to you have not changed. The expectations others have for the type of work you do has not changed. The notifications and distractions in your environment have not changed. Only you have changed. You may have changed your perspective, but others have not changed their expectations.

Recall from the six dimensions that purpose, structures, and resources impact people's abilities to do their jobs. When we clarify our purpose, and help others to understand our purpose, we begin to take steps towards changing others' expectations of us, and when we change expectations, we can do less.

> When we clarify our purpose, and help others to understand our purpose, we begin to take steps towards changing others' expectations of us, and when we change expectations, we can do less.

Remember, I am not suggesting you will have time to stroll in with a cup of coffee, catch up on the news, and then invest hours every day in classroom observations .The goal in changing expectations is to clear a few things off your plate to give yourself a few extra minutes each day. In Stage 4 we'll reinvest those minutes into developing systems which will garner a few additional minutes, and in Stage 5 we will learn to leverage a few precious minutes each day into investing in teacher growth!

In this stage you will learn some simple strategies and techniques to avoid tasks and adjust expectations of the people around you. There are countless ways to achieve these outcomes, but I am going to focus on two:

- *Give it Five* presents a series of five options for off-loading Quadrant 3 tasks. Consistently using these options creates a pattern of intentional decision making to save you a few minutes each day.
- Developing common expectations will make it easier for others to support you and, perhaps, begin a culture shift in your school.

Give it Five

There are things worth doing well. There are also things not worth doing well, things others should do, and things nobody should do. *Give it Five* is a way of thinking through which tasks deserve your and/or others' attention and how much of that attention to give. This doesn't mean being lazy, it means avoiding spending time on Quadrant 3 tasks so you can invest time into Quadrant 2 tasks. *Give it Five* presents a hierarchy of five responses to use when confronted with an "urgent" task, particularly those in Quadrant 3. When encountering such a task, work through each option from top to bottom.

Pause

The most important part of Give it Five is the pause. When a task pops into your space, the first thing to do is to pause. This helps dissipate any emotions which have accumulated throughout the day and set you on the path to being intentional as opposed to reactive. Sometimes we respond to tasks emotionally, especially when we are already in urgent mode. Quadrant 3 isn't just a technical place to be. It is also an emotional place. Some things just feel urgent, but as soon as we pause to reflect, we diminish the emotion, and gain clarity.

Option 1: Give it Up or Do Nothing

Ask yourself whether this is a necessary task. You may be surprised at how many tasks have no impact on safety and teacher growth and aren't required in any rule or policy. Many of these tasks can be ignored. Items in this category include lots of email, especially the FYI types.

This is also an effective strategy for dealing with requests that appear mundane. In some districts it is common practice for people to ask for information they do not need. Yes, I'm serious. The information may be requested in the heat of the moment, with the request being forgotten at a later point in time. When receiving requests to gather data or perform tasks which don't make sense, it can be prudent to do nothing and wait. If the request giver returns, then find out more and complete the request. However, these requests often disappear or evolve, so it can be beneficial to wait.

An additional aspect to giving it up is knowing the difference between the leading edge and the bleeding edge. This largely applies to implementing change initiatives. Jumping onto a new initiative to be in the forefront creates undue stress on the school and the people in it. Remember every "yes" comes with a "no," and if you commit people's time and attention, the two fixed resources, there will be other important things which cannot get done. Being too far out in front can lead to more bleeding than leading.

> Remember every "yes" comes with a "no," and if you commit people's time and attention, the two fixed resources, there will be other important things which cannot get done.

Option 2: Give it Back

Some issues are important to other people but are not important to you or to the organization. These probably shouldn't be ignored as they can impact the invested party's morale, but they also should not become your tasks. You can think of these issues as monkeys. When someone wants to give you their monkey, give it back to them. You don't need to care for other people's monkeys. You can give monkeys back by:

1. Acknowledging the concern and emotions of the monkey owner.
2. Rephrasing the concern as you understand it.
3. Providing them with a task as a next step. The task could include:
   a. Further reflection on the root problem
   b. Developing a list of options
   c. Talking with others
   d. Doing some research
   e. Scheduling a future meeting

Monkeys are particularly dangerous animals to have in schools. I've worked with numerous administrators who became overwhelmed taking care of other people's monkeys. It is easy to fall into the trap of thinking that serving means doing things for people, but this is counterproductive. First, it creates dependency. Instead of doing things for teachers, what if leaders instead focus on helping teachers do things for themselves? The bigger problem is when leaders spend precious time and attention caring for monkeys, they can't invest time and attention in supporting and growing teachers. In the words of Ken Blanchard (2010), "The care and feeding of other people's monkeys is the ultimate lose/lose deal."

These steps help assure the person that you have heard them and validated their concern, but they also put the onus on the person to solve their own problem, or care for their own monkey.

Option 3: Give it Away

You should spend as much time as possible doing what only you can do. This may mean doing what only you have the skill for, but it can also mean doing only what you have the *unique* responsibility to do. There are only a few positions in a school which have teacher development as a primary responsibility: principals, assistant principals, and instructional coaches. Imagine a school with one of each of these positions and forty-eight teachers. When one of these school leaders is doing something not focused on teacher development, at least one teacher will be underserved.

If the task isn't dependent on your unique talent or position, can you give it (delegate) to someone else? This is important as leaders often hang onto or own issues which could be given to others. Some tasks are easy to delegate—you do not need to be the one putting candy bars in every teacher's box or retyping the notes from the MTSS meeting. Others may be more difficult.

There are two things which can limit the use of this strategy. First, people may not complete the task the way you want it completed. For example, front office staff may not format the newsletter exactly the way you would. There are two things you can do. First, accept it. Many times, while the execution may be different, the outcome is every bit as good, if not better. Second, provide a standard operating procedure (SOP) to help guide the person in completing the task. We will look at SOPs in Stage 4.

The second challenge occurs when a person has the potential to complete a task but lacks the skill, knowledge, or both. In this case, a good SOP can provide the support needed to help a person complete the task successfully.

Option 4: Give it a C

This one is difficult for many leaders, which is ironic because it is so easy to execute. If you must be the one to do the task, give it your minimal effort and be done with it. Obviously, this doesn't apply to anything mission critical, but we are specifically addressing Quadrant 3 tasks in this section.

In a previous position I was required to complete an annual report for the state. The report was required but rarely read and had no consequential impact on our program. It was simply a bureaucratic requirement. Each year I duplicated the previous year's report and adjusted any data as necessary. This saved me hours writing a new report each year. And today I could even have artificial intelligence (AI) write the report!

Another example is the semi-annual presentation to the school board. In most districts the presentation serves as an FYI and a chance for the principal or designee to promote their school and accomplishments. However, it doesn't impact funding or other resource allocation. There are principals who spend days preparing the report, when in fact, they could use the same PowerPoint slides as last time with updated data. Think about the impact on teacher growth a principal could have had with all those hours.

What makes this so difficult is our own egos and the conditioning of the educational system. Most of us have been taught to give our best effort and education has taught us to find out what we need to do to get an A. Rarely have we been encouraged to go for a C, but in many situations, it is a wise thing to do.

Option 5: Give it a Bounce

If it is complex and requires your attention, take the minimal action that will allow you to bounce it to someone else for the next step. This gets it off your plate, so you don't need to worry about it. If it comes back to you later, that's fine. Dealing with small tasks is easier than dealing with big ones and a minimal response may be better than a detailed but delayed response.

For example, if you receive an email request for a lengthy amount of information for which you do not have time to gather, send an initial reply that includes the barest minimum of an answer. Then schedule time to follow up into your calendar. Doing so allows you to let go of worrying about getting back the person. And, possibly, your initial email provides enough information that a longer response won't be required.

This is an effective strategy *because incomplete tasks are a distraction.* Once you move the task on, even if it will come back to you, it is at least temporarily out of your hair and will not be a distraction.

Developing Common Expectations

When everyone in the school understands supporting and growing teachers is the most important work, and this kind of work sits in Quadrant 2, then it becomes easier to avoid doing Quadrant 3 work. Investing time in Quadrant 2 becomes easier because there is a common set of expectations.

Developing common expectations involves forging a relationship between word, thought, and deed. Language matters, and the first step to creating common expectations is to teach and use an exact vocabulary. Teach people the meaning and language behind the Eisenhower Matrix, and the different leadership principles of urgent versus strategic leadership.

Help people remember and embrace the language by explaining the concepts and ideas behind the words. When you say you want to prioritize Quadrant 2 work, remind people that is where you help support teachers. When you refer to Quadrant 3 work, help people make the connection that Quadrant 3 prevents you from doing Quadrant 2.

When teachers understand that instead of dealing with office referrals you could be in the classroom helping them figure out how to manage student engagement, they may work more diligently to decrease the number of referrals. When front office staff understand that you are in a classroom helping a teacher to better manage the classroom, and this will mean they could be fielding fewer calls from angry parents, the staff may rethink what "emergencies" warrant calling you out of a classroom.

Bring people to embrace the language and support you by executing deeds. When you recover time from Quadrant 3, immediately invest that time into Quadrant 2. We will look at some key practices for doing that in the next stage.

The key here is consistency. People are not going to remember which Quadrant is which. They aren't going to proactively think about what Quadrant the task is they are asking you to do. They aren't going to naturally think about what you could be doing instead of writing a memo about picking up paper in classrooms at the end of the day. Keep using the language. Post a copy of the Eisenhower Matrix and make your thinking visual. Keep explaining and keep executing.

Over time, consistency in word, thought, and deed, will change the way others behave, which in turn will change the culture of your school. It isn't a magic bullet; it is just patience, consistency, and hard work. And by the way, teachers can use many of these same approaches to help them invest more time in their primary job. Sharing these practices with teachers is a win-win.

Reflection

It's time to check in on Kelli! *Kelli has been able to find a few extra minutes a day by using the five "gives" to spend less time on insignificant work. Specifically, she has turned over some management tasks for the weekly newsletter to front office staff. She has also given some monkeys back to their owners. Kelli is also working on her language. She has shared The Eisenhower Matrix with other leaders and office staff. She talks about spending time in Quadrant 3 and investing time in Quadrant 2. Kelli is vocal in advocating for her role as a developer of teachers, and she is beginning to ask when confronted with an issue, "Is this urgent and important, or is it just urgent?" Kelli is still busy, and still overwhelmed on many days, but she is also finding small chunks of time. But what can she do with five minutes here and five minutes there? She realizes there must be a way to invest those small amounts of time to help her better manage the tasks she has not been able to off load.*

Before moving onto the challenges, reflect on these questions:

1. We looked at the Five Gives. One challenge is executing the Give, but perhaps a bigger challenge is giving ourselves permission to give things up, away, back, a C, and a bounce. Even when we face the reality–thirty minutes spent on something I could have asked someone else to do is thirty minutes I could have invested in supporting an early career teacher–it can feel difficult letting go of some things. How are you feeling about the Five Gives? Have you done any of them already?

2. If you have a task to complete, which is required but not important, and it has little impact, are you able to give it a C? If you consider that the time above a C effort could be invested with a teacher, how does that change how you feel about the C effort?

3. Developing common expectations requires patience and consistency. Are you in a situation where you could, over time, help develop common expectations?

Challenges: Remember the big challenge is required. The other challenges are optional. Do what makes sense given your time, interest, and capacity.

The big challenge

The big challenge this week is to reclaim fifteen minutes of a day:

1. Reclaim 5-10 minutes each day using a combination of strategies from this stage. Choose a couple of key strategies which work for you and which you can continue to execute consistently. For example, you may want to focus on giving people back their monkeys. Whatever seems right for you. Use the experience to develop a package of strategies that can consistently save you a few minutes each day. Remember this is not about time management—it isn't about getting more done. Quite the opposite, this is about getting less done.

Optional challenges

1. Return to your to-do lists from the first or any other week. For all Quadrant 3 items, mentally go through the Five Gives and note which tasks you could have avoided.
2. Monitor all the requests people make of you this week. Be vigilant about not taking other people's monkeys. If someone tries to give you a monkey, give it back. Then reflect on the experience. How did you feel? How did they feel? What can you learn from the experience?
3. Identify a task for which a C is good enough. Give the task a C. Calculate how much time you saved and invest that time with a teacher. Analyze the experience.
4. Print out copies of the Eisenhower Matrix and share them with staff.
5. Schedule and attend a Friday afternoon debrief with your accountability partner.

Stage summary

- There are five strategies to help you avoid spending time on tasks which are not important:
  - Give the task up and ignore it.
  - Give the task back to the person trying to give it to you.
  - Give the task to someone else.
  - Give it the minimal effort required (a C).
  - Give it a bounce by doing one part and then sending to someone else or scheduling time later.
- Developing common expectations involves having discussions about what constitutes important work and what the roles of school leaders should be.

Final reflection

The goal of this stage is to help you protect your time and create more opportunities to invest time in Quadrant 2. Many of the strategies you could implement on your own, but most of them would be far more powerful if you were able to begin changing the culture from one of prioritizing urgent tasks to investing time in supporting and growing people. Reflect:

1. Who in the school would make good allies for reshaping how you approach your work?
2. What sort of resistance did you face in implementing changes? Why did the person/people resist?
3. There are plenty of strategies here that work. You don't need to use all of them. What is the biggest challenge in implementing whichever ones you choose consistently?

Like Kelli, you have been implementing strategies to get to the point where you have a few minutes a day. You have been powering off by decreasing your workload. The next step is to power up by reinvesting saved time into the critical systems which will sustain your new approach and give you a few more minutes each day to focus on supporting and growing your teachers.

STAGE 4

Powering Up

The Question:

Think about the way in which you approach your priorities throughout your day. There are likely things you do which make it more difficult to effectively use your time, and some things you do which make it easier to effectively use your time. What are the practices you use which make it easier, or more difficult to work efficiently?

Goals for Stage 4: Powering Up

1. *Develop processes to make operations more efficient.*
2. *Apply strategies for decreasing interruptions throughout your day.*
3. *Develop common definitions and expectations for "emergencies."*

In Stage 3 I drew the analogy to Apollo 13 when the crew needed to power down all non-essential systems. In their journey, the power conserved was then funneled back to those essential systems so they could last longer. In Stage 3 we looked at powering down by changing people's expectations and avoiding unnecessary tasks. In this stage we will reinvest some of that time in powering up a few critical systems. These systems will improve our usage of time and lead us to the next big stage of igniting our boosters to escape the pull of urgency!

In this stage you will learn some simple strategies and techniques to change the systems around you so you can begin stepping out of Quadrant 3 and into Quadrant 2. Systems can help us or distract us. Luckily, we can build and adapt some of the critical structures which impact our work. There are countless ways to achieve these outcomes. Rather than present an exhaustive list of techniques and strategies, I am going to focus on two easy-to-execute options:

- Standard operating procedures (SOPs) are simple tools which achieve powerful results. SOPs allow you to work more quickly, but their real power comes in supporting other people to perform tasks you might otherwise have had to do yourself.
- Communication hygiene limits the amount and frequency of interruptions which break up your day and slow your pace of work.

Standard Operating Procedures

A standard operating procedure or process (SOP) is a set of directions to help someone perform a task. SOPs can be simple (feed the cat two scoops of food in the morning and at night) or complex (like the ten-page SOP we use for planning, recording, editing, and loading our podcasts). This section on SOPs is not a definitive guide, but there is enough here to get you started.

Some Benefits of SOPs

1. Increase quality of results.
2. Decrease effort and save time.

3. Decrease stress.
4. Ensure compliance with policy.
5. Improve safety.

There is no such thing as a finished SOP. They are living documents, so the way to approach an SOP is to begin it, not complete it. There are five steps to creating an SOP:

1. Identify the priorities. Why write an SOP? How will you know if it is successful?
2. Identify the first step. When does the procedure begin?
3. Identify the end point. When is the procedure complete?
4. Map the A-B steps from the first step to the final one.
5. Implement, monitor, and adjust.

Using a minimally viable process (MVP) approach, simply getting something down on paper is a win. Steps 1-5 should take a minimum amount of time. The SOP doesn't need to be good, just good enough to test. Step 5 is the critical step for creating a better procedure over time but deploying something flawed will have a bigger immediate impact than spending six months developing a modern wonder of engineering precision.

Let's look at an example. When the world moved into a virtual space in March 2020, Zoom meetings became a daily occurrence. Invariably I would jump on a meeting, turn on my camera and notice my hair was out of place, or my glasses were on (I don't need them for Zoom meetings), or I didn't have what I needed pulled up on my desktop, or I had too much on my desktop, or, worst of all, I forgot to turn on my mic.

Before each meeting, I would try and remember all the things needing to be in place. This was stressful and time consuming and about 50% of the time I forgot to do something. Then I heard someone talking about their SOP for virtual meetings and decided I also needed one.

My initial SOP went like this:

- Check your appearance.
- Have water.
- Silence all notifications.
- Turn on mic.
- Set desk height to memory 1. (I have an adjustable desk)

I added the SOP document to the dock in my computer so I could open it with a single click before any meeting. I would run down the list and be ready for my meeting. This was an improvement. Each time I found an issue I added it to the document. Additions included:

- Letting everyone in the house know when I was on a meeting, so they didn't barge into my office.
- *"Turn on mic!!!"* in bold italics with exclamation points because I kept forgetting.
- Separate "turn off notifications" prompts for my phone and my computer.
- A whole wrap-up section to guide me through closing out the meeting and letting the rest of the house know I was done.

Even now I continue to tweak the SOP as I change equipment or software.

For the purposes of intentional leadership, writing SOPs will help you:

- Consistently complete tasks with more fidelity and less stress and effort.
- Train others to complete tasks you would have otherwise had to do yourself.

Important SOPs include the following:

- Completing formal evaluations.
- Following up on discipline referrals.
- Greeting parents who do not have an appointment.
- Conducting audits and inventory.
- Creating newsletters or other informational items.
- Opening of school.
- Creating the master schedule.

SOPs save you time by helping you do things faster and more accurately, so you do not have to return to a task to fix a mistake. Also, because they are a specific set of step-by-step instructions, they can help you train other people to do part or all of a task which you would otherwise have to do. An SOP for dealing with parents who show up without an appointment **empowers your staff,** protects your time for growing teachers, and should lead to happier parents.

Communication Hygiene

There are books on managing your communications. There are also communication gurus, of which I am not one. I'm going to keep this section simple and provide a handful of strategies for managing your communications. If you would like to draw on other sources for more advanced techniques, feel free to do so.

Good communication hygiene achieves two things. First, it decreases the number of interruptions and distractions you receive throughout the day. Second, it helps you stay fully present when you are with others.

Think about any of the essential things you do, such as working with a challenging student, coaching a teacher, or meeting with a team.

Imagine getting a call or text or having your email alert go off. What happens? Every interruption in such an activity has multiple negative effects:

- Disrupts your train of thought.
- Slows mental processing.
- Increases stress.
- Increases the chance of making a mistake.
- Disrupts flow state and inhibits creativity.
- Increases cognitive load resulting in increased fatigue.

Good communication hygiene achieves two things. First, it decreases the number of interruptions and distractions you receive throughout the day. Second, it helps you stay fully present when you are with others.

Worst of all, when you are with another person and your notifications intrude, your presence is diminished. Checking your notifications in the presence of another person sends a subtle but powerful message that they are not as important as whoever or whatever sent you the notification. In the three epiphany terms, your choice to focus on the message instead of the person communicates you value tasks over people.

Even a simple distraction, like a banner or ping, can cost up to thirty seconds of productivity, and subsequent interruptions have increasingly negative effects. A long series of interruptions degrades our ability to work effectively or efficiently.

Managing communications means preventing unwanted interruptions while you are doing the important work in Quadrant 2. It also means being able to carve out uninterrupted time to complete

Quadrant 1 tasks and the inevitable unavoidable Quadrant 3 tasks. Communications hygiene limits interruptions and increases the ability to do meaningful work. It includes three aspects that complement each other:

1. Setting boundaries
2. Managing expectations
3. Eliminating distractions

Boundaries

1. Block out times to do the following:
   a. Observe, conference, coach, and listen to teachers
   b. Perform administrative and managerial tasks
2. Do not allow interruptions for anything other than emergencies during these blocked times.
3. Set aside 2-3 chunks of time to look at email. Email is not a to-do list. If there are people who expect you to be available on email, tell them you don't use email for that purpose and explain your reasoning.
4. Check out the basic email tips at the end of this chapter or from another source. Follow as many as you can.

In creating boundaries, it is essential to work with other school leaders and office/admin staff.

Covering Emergencies

Coordination within the leadership team makes covering emergencies much easier. When leadership teams meet regularly and schedule blocks of time to complement each other, emergencies become less of a problem. Try the following:

- Coordinate time blocks so each team member has dedicated blocks of time to support and grow teachers and to complete important managerial tasks.
- Protect these blocks by designating someone to be "on call" for emergencies.
- Rotate coverage so each team member has uninterrupted time each day.
- Share the schedule with front office staff.
- Work with the entire staff to define what constitutes an emergency. Begin with examining what issues are more important than supporting and growing teachers.
- Use an SOP to help train teachers to go through the front office for emergencies.

Managing Expectations

- Define what an emergency is (a safety situation in which someone faces serious bodily harm).
- Teach everyone what your definition of an emergency is. An angry parent is not an emergency. They are important, but they are not an emergency.

- Identify ONE communication method for use during an emergency. When in school, I suggest that form of contact is someone from the front office physically coming to you to inform you of the situation. By increasing the effort required to interrupt you, the frequency of interruptions should decrease.
- Control access by limiting the number of people who can interrupt you for emergencies, for example the principal and the lead office administrator.
- Use email sparingly. Condition people within your building that if they want something from you, they should come and find you, not send you an email. Email makes it easy for people to ask us to do things with little to no effort on their part.

You can increase support for staff by collaborating with them to develop SOPs for a variety of situations. For example, an SOP for asking an upset parent to schedule an appointment might include specific verbal phrases and a process that allows the parent to express their concerns without interacting immediately with an administrator. Some leaders may balk at not meeting with angry parents immediately, but as a former principal and current associate superintendent said to me, "They [parents] calm down later when you talk to them, or they go to the district office, but the district can't complain about you being in classes."

Eliminating Distractions

1. Create notification gatekeepers.
2. Mute all notifications.
3. Use do not disturb functions on your devices.

Create gatekeepers to limit who has access to you during specific times. Modern smartphones allow you to build customized "do not disturb" settings to tailor who can reach you in specific situations. Create a setting for when you are with teachers that allows the bare minimum of people to reach you. Those people become gatekeepers, allowing only significant "emergencies" from interrupting time you have scheduled with teachers.

Mute all your notifications. If you program your devices to allow messages from your gatekeepers, you can then turn off everything else. This includes silent notifications like banners and the red bubbles that appear on apps. You do not need to know how many emails are piling up while you help a new teacher learn to manage a talkative student.

It may not be possible to implement all these practices, especially if you are an AP and your principal or district leaders hold different expectations. However, much of the harm done by our abuse of communications is self-inflicted. If a cell phone is not the preferred method of emergency communication, don't bring it with you when you are greeting students in the morning. You don't need your email notifications when you are conferencing with a teacher. Cell phones can be programmed to ring through even on silent if specific people call twice in a row. Use this functionality to concurrently limit and allow access.

Some of these strategies may seem out of reach, but one of the best principals I know rarely replies to email. If I want to speak with him, I call him after school hours, because during the day he is in classrooms or with people. He has never lost his job because he didn't respond to email. In fact, he has been sought after continuously because he has earned a reputation for turning around schools by supporting and growing teachers. I can imagine him responding to criticism from higher up with a question: "Did you hire me to answer emails or to build a better school?"

Reflection

Kelli has begun reinvesting some of her saved time from Stage 3 into structures and systems which will help protect more of her time and make it easier for her to stay focused on her priorities. Kelli has devoted 5-10 minutes each day to reflect on and improve the procedures around discipline referrals. She has worked with grade-level teacher leaders to clarify the process for office referrals and share it with teachers. This has resulted in a small but noteworthy decrease in the number of referrals. Kelli has also worked with her principal and office administrator to develop an SOP for office referrals and communicated to staff that students removed from class should be sent to the office administrator, not the assistant principal.

As a result, Kelli has been able to examine the discipline data and identify specific teachers, students, and times for the most frequent issues. She has been able to conduct more walk-throughs and do some brief targeted observations. Kelli is still busy, but she has learned to prioritize a few tasks each day and the progress she is making is now allowing her to move to prioritizing something even more important: people!

Now Kelli is prioritizing building relationships with two of her teachers who struggle most with discipline. Ms. Marple is a veteran teacher who has had multiple traumas in her personal life over the past three years and is struggling to bring all of herself into the classroom each day. Ms. Jenna is a first-year teacher coming from an alternative certification program. She asks for feedback and help but has struggles to follow up on suggestions.

Before moving onto the challenges, reflect on these questions:

1. SOPs are common practice in some fields like medicine, but not as common in education. What applications do you see for using SOPs? What is the biggest challenge for implementing them?

2. Our relationship with email, and some other forms of communication, has passed the boundary of treating them like a utilitarian tool. We have added meaning and power to these forms beyond what is reasonable. How much does email influence your ability to do meaningful work? How much does it

influence how you live your life?

3. If all the administrators were out of the building and unavailable, what would constitute an emergency so important that someone would call the district office? Who would handle the "emergencies" which didn't warrant a call to the DO?

4. We've looked at limiting communications at work, but what's happening in your life away from work? How are you managing those communications?

Challenges: Remember the big challenge is required. The other challenges are optional. Do what makes sense given your time, interest, and capacity.

The big challenge

The big challenge this week has two parts:

+ Invest 5- 15 minutes each day in creating an SOP for a function which you do frequently.
+ Look for opportunities to off load part of that function onto someone else using the SOP.
+ Tweak the SOP as needed.
+ Have conversations with the rest of your team about SOPs you have or need and consider developing them collaboratively.
+ Check email no more than three times a day.

Optional challenges

1. Critically examine your discipline SOP. If you don't have one, create one. Make sure it includes directions for teachers on the front end. The discipline SOP should make it crystal clear what the steps will be. The first two steps should resemble

something like:

    a.   Teacher conferences with student about the behavior

    b.   Teacher contacts parents about the behavior

2. Reach out to other school leaders in your district and ask for copies of their SOPs.

3. Block two or three chunks of time in your calendar to work on email. Don't look at email outside of those times. Do this for one or more days.

4. Manage who can contact you on your phone when you are in classrooms or working with teachers.

5. Silence all notifications for email, texts, and other apps.

6. Schedule and attend a Friday afternoon debrief with your accountability partner.

Stage summary

+ Standard operating procedures (SOPs) help tasks be completed more quickly and accurately and can be an important tool in delegating tasks to others.
+ Communications hygiene includes:
  ◦ Establishing boundaries for who can access you and when.
  ◦ Clearly defining what constitutes an emergency.
  ◦ Blocking time to devote to specific tasks.
  ◦ Turning off notifications settings.

Final reflection

The goal of this stage is to help you create more opportunities to invest time in Quadrant 2. Many of the strategies you could implement on your own, but most of them would be more powerful if you were able to begin changing the culture from one of prioritizing urgent tasks to investing time in supporting and growing people. Reflect:

1. Who in the school would make good allies for reshaping how we approach our work?
2. What sort of resistance did you face in implementing changes? Why did the person/people resist?
3. There are plenty of strategies here that work. You don't need to use all of them. What is the biggest challenge in implementing whichever ones you choose consistently?

In Stage 2 we learned that time management is not the issue, and that priority management is the key to escaping the gravitational pull of urgency. That doesn't mean that time management is not important, only that it is not enough. As you implement systems and strategies to keep yourself out of Quadrant 3, time management strategies become more valuable. As you incorporate time management strategies you can recover even more minutes from Quadrant 1 or from those Quadrant 3 tasks that you cannot avoid.

We saw how Kelli has saved a few minutes each day and reinvested those minutes into systems to pay even larger dividends. With some of the systems work completed, Kelli can focus that saved time on teachers and so can you. But what can you do to grow teachers in only 5-15 minutes a day?

In Stage 6 we will look at how to create a proactive system to maximize the benefits of that time, but the more critical thing to do right now is to invest those precious minutes into some simple practices that will provide the extra burst you need to propel you out of the urgency's gravitational pull and into space, towards your destination.

STAGE 5

The Slingshot

The Question

Think about your growth as a teacher and as a leader. Can you remember small conversations that led to significant growth? When did those conversations take place and with whom? What made them powerful?

Goals for Stage 5: The Slingshot

1. *Develop skills to empower being fully present.*
2. *Learn to ask a second question that demonstrates care.*
3. *Master the practice of using reflective questions.*

At this point you are beginning to escape the pull of urgency. But you aren't there yet. In fact, you may have been here before, and therein lies a risk. By approaching your work differently, implementing habits, and building systems, you should be recovering a few minutes a day. If you have ever concentrated on applying time management and efficiency strategies, you may have experienced brief moments when you felt you had it all under control, only to have it come crashing down.

The crew of Apollo 13 must have felt the same way. They were getting back on course, but needed just a bit more to get them there. They made minor adjustments to their direction by using small amounts of fuel to get them pointed in the right direction at the right time. Similarly, you now have a small allotment of fuel (time) with which to make sure you are pointed in the right direction.

Remember!

Time management is not the issue.
The issue is priority management.
Time management doesn't work if you use
it as a tool to do more.
It works when you use it to do the right
things more efficiently.

With priority management, you have put the important things (Quadrants 1 and 2) first. Now the challenge is to take the time you saved in Quadrant 3 and invest it into Quadrant 2 for maximum effect. Reinvesting time into teacher support and growth serves as a slingshot which accelerates the journey towards strategic leadership because it develops the foundational strategies and habits of being a strategic leader.

Let's be realistic. Even with your efforts to engage in priority management, to build systems, use habits, and manage expectations, you are still only recovering a few minutes a day. This is not a magic bullet. So, how do you impact your school with just a few minutes each day? In this stage, we will begin implementing two high-leverage practices. These practices offer the following benefits:

+ They are simple.
+ They compound over time, achieving a long-lasting positive impact.
+ They are short, requiring only minutes to successfully execute.

Being Present

The single most powerful gifts you can give are your time and attention. Remember these are the two resources that can never increase–they are static. For that reason, they are the most valuable. Understand these are two separate gifts, but their value increases exponentially when they are given together.

If you have ever been with someone physically but could see they were distracted and thinking about other things, then you understand. The person gave you their time, but not their full attention. When we give all our attention to someone, and are physically with them, then we are fully present.

There are two challenging parts of being present. The first challenge is to bring your full attention. In a world that moves so quickly and is so demanding, it can be very difficult to focus fully on someone else. Here are some of the specific ways that our attention drifts when we are trying to be present:

+ We think about what we are doing next or later.
+ We begin thinking about what we will say when the person finishes talking.
+ We react to something and begin focusing on our emotions.
+ We get distracted by the piece of spinach in their teeth, or their hair sticking straight up.

We can use presence in multiple ways but at this stage we are going to focus on two specific ways to leverage the power of presence.

Responsive Presence

First, we want to be fully present when people seek us out. We can refer to this as responsive presence. When people are coming to you, they are usually interrupting you. I don't say that to be harsh, only factual. You are always doing something, so if someone comes to you, they are necessarily interrupting something you are trying to accomplish. The challenge is for you to let go of the task that has been interrupted. Here are the keys to responsive presence:

- Increase physical proximity by eliminating barriers, moving closer, and fully facing the person. Use furniture that minimizes physical and power distances, such as a small round table instead of a long rectangular one.
- Put down and/or step away from anything that can distract you like your phone or computer.
- Take a deep breath and exhale out the task you had been working on.
- Look the person in the eyes (unless culturally inappropriate), listen, and smile.
- Focus intently on what they are saying, specifically on the meaning of what they are saying.
- Ask clarification questions if necessary.
- Just listen—yes…don't talk.

In responsive presence, we can assume that someone wants something. Maybe it is to share a celebration. Something great happened and they want to talk about it. Or maybe they have an issue or feeling that they just need to verbally process. It isn't that they need you to solve their problem, they just need to talk it through to solve it themselves. In these two cases, your presence is giving them exactly what they need. Resist the urge to speak, advise, or "add value" when the most precious value comes from your presence.

In other instances, people may want you to do something. It may be to answer a question, in which case you can answer the question. And then be quiet. They may want you to do something, at which point you can consider what quadrant the task is in and begin working through the Five Gives. Note that if you aren't fully present, it is much more difficult to be discerning, and you will wind up taking on unnecessary tasks. It feels counterintuitive, but stopping long enough to be fully present saves you time.

Being present is about giving to the other person. If we are speaking, we aren't giving. To the greatest extent possible, just listen and learn. By listening, we will learn what others need from us. One thing I struggle with is mixing up my own need to share with an effort to connect. The person talks about their cat, and I jump in to tell my cat story. I tell myself that I am sharing the story to connect, when in reality I just want to talk about myself and my cat. As cool as my cat is, listening to their story and asking a powerful question would build more connection than a quid-pro-quo exchange of stories.

> Being present is about giving to the other person. If we are speaking, we aren't giving.

As a side note, there are times when you should not be interrupted. Many leaders like to have an open-door policy and that's nice, but leaders should also have a closed-door policy. If you have thirty minutes budgeted to finish a report or deal with email, shut your door and take care of the tasks. You don't need to be responsive 100% of the time.

Proactive Presence

When we seek out others to be present with, we are engaging in proactive presence. Proactive presence occurs when we go to someone else to specifically give them the gift of our presence. If I am visiting someone to take care of a task or get an answer to a question, that is not proactive presence because I am arriving with an agenda. Proactive presence has only one agenda–to be with someone to support them or to learn more about them. Proactive presence is the building block of relationships.

We can execute proactive presence in different ways, but the simplest technique is called *asking the second question*. It works this way:

+ Ask a question.
+ Be quiet and listen.
+ Based on their response, ask the next question.
+ Be quiet and listen.

The goal of asking the second question is twofold:

1. Show them you value them by listening.
2. Show them you are listening by asking the second question.

The simplest way to practice asking the second question is with the ubiquitous "How are you?" It goes like this:

+ You: "How are you?"
+ Them: "Fine."
+ You: "OK, really, how are you?"
+ Them: "..."
+ You: "..."
+ Them: "To be honest, I'm feeling..."

We have been conditioned to inquire as to people's state of well-being by asking "How are you?" At the same time, we have also been trained that this is merely a polite thing to ask. As such, most people understand that when you ask, "How are you?" you don't actually want to know how they are doing. You are just being polite. So, they respond with the polite answer, which is "Fine."

When we ask the second question, we are signaling to the other person that we do want to know the answer. With the second question we communicate care, and with our presence we create the space for people to share and process. Our presence is the gift, and it is the most precious of gifts because it consists of the two things we can never create more of – time and attention.

Caution!

Asking the second question is about giving the other person the space. As soon as you open your mouth to speak, you are taking back space, and this can have a negative impact. We have been conditioned to paraphrase and to provide feedback, but those take away from the precious gifts of time and attention. Just be quiet.

I was once working with a new principal. It was mid-fall and we had only met in person one time, at the beginning of the year in August. Eight weeks later we met on a Zoom call, and I asked, "How are you?" and she said, "Good, good, everything is going well." But I was fully present, so I heard the slight hesitation, the small inflection, that hinted that there was more here. So, I asked the second question. "Really, how are you?" And she burst into tears. We sat quietly for a few minutes. I didn't say anything—this was her time and I wanted to honor her emotions by accepting them, not trying to "fix" them.

Much later we moved onto other topics, but the value of the session came from her being able to share what was happening and how she was feeling. I was able to affirm that value by just listening. I didn't try to tell her how she should feel, or what the future would be like. I just listened.

I tell this story because my biggest fear is that you ask the second question, open something profound, and then begin talking or trying to fix it. Please understand—the gift is the presence, the space you create by being attentive and giving your time. As soon as you speak, you are taking that gift away. People don't need your encouragement or your advice. They need you to listen, without judgment, without feedback. Just ask the second question, and then be quiet.

There are a few people who will take advantage of your ability and willingness to be present. Some of these people are so focused on themselves they fail to appreciate the value of presence. They are likely to use such a gift not for reflection of processing, but rather for a laundry list of grievances or complaints. Others are interested in company and someone to spend their time with. Again, these people fail to appreciate the value of presence. Here are two simple strategies for handling such people:

- Limit the amount of time you give them by saying "I can give you five minutes of my undivided attention" and then set a timer on your phone. When the timer goes off, excuse yourself. The timer is helpful as it interrupts the conversation for you.
- Tell them you can't meet with them this instant and ask them if you can get back to them at a specific future time which is convenient for you and inconvenient for them, or which will have a hard stop (e.g. five minutes before classes begin).

Of course, not every episode is going to lead to an intense emotional experience. Perhaps the most common response to asking the second question is "No, really, I'm fine." But simply by asking, you have given the person something special. Occasionally, you will create space for someone who really needs it, and instead of giving something special, you will be giving something beyond value.

Five-Minute Coaching

Five-minute coaching (5-mc) is an extension of proactive presence. Labeling it coaching might be a bit misleading, because it isn't like coaching in the sense of providing feedback. As with other forms of presence, listening is more important than talking. The coaching aspect occurs because you are helping the teacher reflect on their own teaching. Reflection is the most powerful form of professional development, so five-minute coaching is a critical way to support teacher growth.

Five-minute coaching has some distinct benefits:

1. You need only five minutes, not the 30-60 required for a "real" coaching session.
2. It shows teachers you are invested in their growth.
3. It helps them become more reflective practitioners.
4. It helps them connect specific actions to specific results to improve future performance.
5. It can provide you with information you would not have otherwise received.
6. It helps you become better at being fully present.

You can conduct a five-minute coaching session after a specific event such as a lesson, meeting, presentation, phone call, or completion of a project. 5-mc is meant to be informal, so don't take notes! The best place to do 5-mc is at a teacher's door, standing in the classroom, or walking in the hallway. You can plan to do 5-mc or do it impromptu, but it should feel spontaneous and unrehearsed.

A five-minute coaching session begins with you standing face-to-face or side-by-side a teacher and then doing this:

1. Make an affirming statement: "I enjoyed being in your classroom today."
2. Ask: "What went well?"
3. Be quiet, listen, smile, and nod.
4. Ask: "Did anything surprise you?"
5. Be quiet, listen, smile, and nod.
6. Ask: "Is there anything you would do differently next time?"
7. Be quiet, listen, smile, and nod.
8. Say something optimistic: "I'm excited to see what you do next!"
9. Thank them for sharing: "Thanks for sharing."

That's all it is, but there are three challenges in 5-mc:

- Memorizing the questions so they feel natural.
- Staying present.
- Remaining quiet.

Let's take a deeper look into the process. The questions are asked in a specific way for a specific purpose. As you become more practiced, you can try adapting the questions, but always keep in mind that you want the questions to be as open ended and inviting as possible.

Begin with a Statement of Optimism

Beginning with a statement of optimism sets a positive tone and shows that you value them. With enthusiastic sincerity and a big smile, say: "I appreciate the work you are doing with x" or "The kids were having so much fun with that activity yesterday!"

You can increase value by connecting a concrete action to a positive outcome: "When you (observed behavior) the impact was (result)." For example, "When you incorporated movement, I saw students who were normally more passive become fully engaged."

What Went Well?

Beginning the reflection by focusing on positives puts the teacher into a positive mindset.

Say: "What <u>else</u> went well?" Using "else" indicates that you are building on the affirmation and that this process is about accentuating the positives. If you didn't lead off the conversation by acknowledging a success, just drop the "else." If you want to hear more, you can say "Tell me more" but do not ask specific questions. This will interfere with the reflection and take control away from the teacher. Part of the power of the questions is they allow the teacher to control the conversation.

Surprises

Asking about surprises is like opening a door. It presents an opportunity to go somewhere different, but the teacher doesn't need to walk through the door. It is a powerful reflection question because it allows teachers to work through an entire lesson looking for surprises. Most of us will make note of what goes well and what doesn't when we execute a task, but considering what surprised us helps us revisit the entirety of the task from a different perspective.

Say: "Did anything surprise you?" Sometimes "nothing" is a legitimate answer. Even if you disagree, accept it, and move on. Using "Did anything surprise you?" instead of "What surprised you?" gives teachers an easy out, which increases comfort and trust.

Changes

This question is about what they would do differently. It doesn't need to be a negative.

Say: "Would you do anything differently next time?" Again, using "Would you?" instead of "What would you?" gives them an easy out. If they say nothing, accept it and move on.

Conclusion

A positive statement of optimism ends the conference on a positive note.

Say: "Thank you so much for sharing x with me, and please let me know what I can do to continue to support your work and growth."

You can increase the power of 5-minute coaching by being transparent. This may be especially important if teachers are not accustomed to you asking them about their teaching. You can:

+ Let teachers know you are developing your coaching skills by doing 5-mc.
+ Tell them you want to be a better listener and won't be giving feedback.
+ Tell them you will try to get to each person every few days.
+ Ask them to help by reminding you.

This technique of transparency was shared with me by a principal I had been coaching. She used it when she first began using 5-minute coaching. She told me after a few days teachers were asking her expectantly, "Are you going to coach me today?"

Being transparent helps teachers understand you won't be giving feedback and you are trying to be a better listener. Also, by making your growth goals transparent, *you are modeling the growth mindset we want kids and teachers to have.* Finally, asking for help is a great way to get teachers to invest in the process.

Frequently asked questions:

- **What if something was bad but the teacher won't talk about it?** It's OK. If they aren't ready to go there, then they aren't ready to grow from it and 5-mc is about their growth.
- **What if there was something they should change, but they don't talk about it?** Same as above. Five-minute coaching allows teachers to reflect at the level they are at. Just stay consistent and eventually they will go deeper. Remember, many teachers have been traumatized by or are intimidated by administrators. They may not feel comfortable being transparent. *Your acceptance is one way to build trust.*
- **What if they ask for feedback?** Don't give them feedback. If they are insistent, tell them, "This is about you, for you, and I want you to indulge in self-reflection. If there is something specific you want to talk about, let's schedule a separate time."
- **Should you ever write anything down?** If you hear something you need to remember, write it down after the session is over. For example, if a teacher shares they have an ill parent or child. Put it on your calendar for a few days later and come back and ask them about it.
- **What if I don't have five minutes?** You don't have to ask all three questions. If you do 5-mc regularly, you can skip questions but still give teachers the chance to reflect. In schools where leaders consistently use 5-mc, teachers begin to answer the questions before they are asked—which is the whole point.

With limited time, being present for everyone will be impossible, but presence is an investment which yields compound interest. Being consistently present with a teacher fosters a deeper relationship and trust, in addition to developing self-reflection skills. All three of these things will continue to pay future dividends, so choosing who to focus on can be a conundrum.

> Being consistently present with a teacher fosters a deeper relationship and trust, in addition to developing self-reflection skills.

Consider these factors:

- What is your comfort level with being present?
- With whom will this be easiest?
- Is there someone who is already good at reflecting?
- Who might profit most from self-reflection?
- Who do you most need to enhance your relationship with?
- Who most needs to feel a stronger relationship with you?

It is fine to focus on being present with people who are easy to be present with while you practice and sharpen your skills. Don't feel rushed to take a risk or engage with someone who might provide challenges. You can work with more challenging people when you are ready, and you don't need to force it.

At the time I was writing this guide, my adult son Collin got a puppy named Ruby. The thing about dogs is they are always fully present. As Collin cuddled and played with his new friend, they didn't need to have a conversation to feel joy. Ruby doesn't need to give Collin feedback to make him feel important. She just needs to be present. And she is.

As you work through this week, remember the power of presence is the gift of your time and attention. Staying silent lets the people you are with take full advantage of the gift. Even when people ask you to comment, you can simply respond with, "What do you think?"

Reflection

When we left Kelli in Stage 4, she had been able to reflect and learn more about her teachers' needs. While the priority management and alignment strategies have helped her recover some time, she still must be judicious. Kelli has chosen to focus on being fully present with two teachers. As she works to become more present, she encounters different reactions from her teachers. Ms. Jenna, the first-year teacher, is effusive. Initially her reflections are at a surface level, but she enjoys the five-minute coaching format. At first, Ms. Jenna asks for feedback, but Kelli reminds her that this is the teacher's time, not the administrator's. As time passes, Ms. Jenna embraces the five-minute coaching opportunities and begins to reflect more deeply on her own practice and can identify her struggles clearly. After several weeks, at the end of a five-minute coaching session, Jenna asks Kelli for help with classroom management. She says, "I need you to tell me what to do."

In contrast, the veteran teacher, Ms. Marple, is initially resistant to five-minute coaching. She always responds with "nothing" to the questions about surprises and changes and seems disinterested during the sessions. However, several times, when asking the second question, "Really, how are you?" Ms. Marple has opened up about deeply personal issues, including her father's battle with dementia. Over time, Kelli learns to read Ms. Marple's emotional states and proactively reaches out with affirming support during low times. Eventually Ms. Marple begins responding to five-minute coaching more deeply. Kelli learns how Ms. Marple is trying to juggle care for her father with her teaching responsibilities, and how she questions her value as both a daughter and a teacher, and how little she has been able to sleep over the past 18 months.

Before moving onto the challenges, reflect on these questions:

1. Is it difficult to embrace the idea that your silence is more valuable than your words? What experiences have you had which challenge this idea? What experiences have you had which confirm it?

2. Imagine you see three weaknesses in a lesson, and you point them out to the teacher. Alternatively, the teacher identifies one thing they want to work more on, and it isn't one of the weaknesses you saw. Would it be more valuable for the teacher to focus on what they want, or to adapt to what you want?

Challenges: Remember the big challenge is required. The other challenges are optional. Do what makes sense given your time, interest, and capacity.

The big challenge

The big challenge this week is:

1. Pick between one and three people and tell them the following:
   * You are focusing on being present this week.
   * You will do this in two ways, by asking reflective questions and by listening.
   * You need their help in being accountable and you want them to monitor your progress and check in with you on Wednesday and Friday afternoons.
   * Explain that time and attention are the two most valuable resources, and because you value the people, you want to give those resources to them.
   * Assure the people the only thing you are asking for in return is their feedback on Wednesday and Friday.
   * Explain that you are reading these directions from a list because that's what the guide said to do.

2. Each day, check in with each person *twice*. One time ask the second question. One time engage in five-minute coaching. Every day. If you have only five minutes a day, only choose one person. If you have fifteen minutes, choose three people. Less is more. You can always practice being present with people other than the ones you recruit.

3. On Wednesday and Friday, meet briefly with your teachers and ask for feedback. Specifically:

   - Thank you for helping me grow by encouraging me to be fully present with you.
   - In terms of me being present with you, what has gone well?
   - Were there any surprises?
   - Is there anything I could do differently?

If there is a specific response you want to follow up on, simply say, "Tell me more." Of course, you see what we've done here. By using the three questions as a basis for feedback you are encouraging them to think deeply about the process which allows them to provide you with better feedback.

4. Throughout the week, monitor what is happening with you:

   - How difficult is it to be attentive when being present? What kind of thoughts are the most intrusive?
   - How do you feel at the end of each episode of being present? More frantic or calmer? Drained or energized? Pessimistic or optimistic?
   - Do you learn any important information during the week which you probably would not have discovered without being present?
   - Does your relationship with the teachers change?

Optional challenges

1. Monitor every conversation you have in a single day. For each conversation reflect on whether the other person was fully present with you.

2. Monitor others' behavior in every conversation. How many times do people look at their phones or a computer screen while you are talking? How does it make you feel?

3. Monitor what happens when people ask you, "How are you?"
   a. How many times do they ask but not listen to the answer?
   b. How many times do you give them the true answer?
   c. When you don't provide the true answer, why don't you?
   d. What would they need to do to get you to give the true answer?

4. Do a five-minute coaching session with a teacher you know is struggling and who you suspect will not be open to reflection. Check your mindset going in—no matter how shallow the teacher's responses are, you will not give any feedback. Do five-minute coaching with the teacher three times during the week. This teacher can be included in the main challenge. Monitor the teacher's responses and your own thoughts and feelings. Is there a change between the first and third session?

5. Schedule and attend a Friday afternoon debrief with your accountability partner.

Stage summary

- The key to responsive presence is to stop, let go of other thoughts and tasks, and focus on listening.
- Asking the second question involves asking a question a second time to communicate that you really want to hear the true and full answer to the question.

- Five-Minute Coaching consists of asking three reflective questions and listening to the answers without providing feedback.

Final reflection

The goal of this stage is to help you learn to reinvest small chunks of time to achieve maximum impact by being fully present with teachers. Most of your reflection should have occurred during your check-ins with the teachers you chose to be present with, but here are a couple other things to reflect on:

1. Outside of time, what will be the biggest barrier to continuing to be present?
2. How can you account for those barriers?
3. Have you noticed any spill over in your ability to be present outside of school?

By investing small chunks of time being present, you have begun to increase your impact on people in your school, and this is the power which slingshots you away from urgency and back onto the journey you originally set out on. People are at the heart of *Strategic Leadership* and focusing on people at this stage has primed you to move into the stage of *Strategic Leadership*.

STAGE 6

Strategic Leadership

The Question:

What does the school look like when it is centered around the health, well-being, and capacity of teachers? How might that be different from the school you work in?

Goals for Stage 6: Strategic Leadership

1. *Understand the two ways to help people: growth and support.*
2. *Learn the formula for motivating people.*
3. *Examine the benefits of incremental change.*

Before going any further, I have a confession. When I began writing my first book, this is not the book I had intended to write. I wanted to write a book to teach school leaders to redesign their systems and resources towards the purpose of supporting and growing their teachers. However, while leaders are stuck doing the urgent leadership in Quadrant 3, they cannot engage in *Strategic Leadership* in Quadrant 2. Out of necessity, this guide was born.

I share this now in this chapter on *Strategic Leadership* to explain that this stage is a book unto itself, and in this guide, we are just scratching the surface of *Strategic Leadership*.

To return to the space journey analogy, stages one through five of this guide have taken you into view of your destination—Stage 6. Stage 6 is its own journey, but here I will explain the four principles of *Strategic Leadership* and include a few practices for applying them.

Strategic Leadership

Strategic Leadership focuses on a systemic approach to supporting and growing teachers. It is the application of four core principles to daily action. These principles are:

1. People before tasks.
2. Purpose and priorities ahead of urgency and time.
3. Problem identification instead of treating symptoms.
4. Progress and incremental changes matter more than action.

People

When comparing *Strategic Leadership* to urgent leadership, I talk about putting people before tasks. We must be people-oriented if we are going to prioritize the right things. Within the *Strategic Leadership* framework itself, I also put people before purpose.

This may sound a bit backwards at first, but it is the way we should be leading schools. In the six dimensions framework we discussed people. Specifically, we noted people have four attributes of knowledge, skills, dispositions, and health. We have also noted better teachers equal better schools.

Unfortunately, putting purpose before people focuses the organization on outcome measures. In education, this means standardized test results. When we look at "how to increase test scores" we take the focus off people. We might make the link back by analyzing test data, associating a teaching weakness to a specific score deficiency, and then doing professional development (PD) on the strategy. But this is still not a focus on the teacher as a person. Providing PD to increase the score on a specific aspect of a test treats teachers like factory machines. If we fine tune the machine, then our quality control indicators will improve. Strategic leaders understand this, so they choose to put people before purpose. When we put people first, we become partners in helping them grow to fulfill their priorities. This creates professional growth in which we work side by side instead of top down.

Throughout this stage, I will reference "the work" of teachers. Teachers are responsible for helping to grow young people, so those people grow into adults who have agency in their lives. This is the true purpose of schooling, and for teachers, "the work" is about growing those young people. The vast majority of teachers understand this inherently, and they don't need mission statements, mantras, test scores, or marketing to focus them on the importance of their work. Centering teachers and their work focuses us on what is truly important, because teachers know what is truly important!

Working with people has three parts: support, growth, and care.

Support: Supporting people involves improving alignment within the school, because misalignment is largely responsible for the barriers teachers face in doing the work. Remember back to the six dimensions of organizations. Misalignment can happen in multiple ways:

- The structures (physical, legible, and intangible) act as barriers, making it more difficult for people to do their work.
- The resources (dynamic and static) are disproportionately allocated so they do not support teachers' work.

- The purpose is unclear or inconsistent with teachers' understanding of their work.
- Teachers lack knowledge, skills, dispositions, and or the health capacity to engage in the work.

By attending to school structures leaders create an environment that works with teachers instead of against them.

Growth: I noted back in Stage 2 that the path to school improvement lies in developing stronger teachers. Strategic leaders focus their work and the organization on developing teachers by building a flywheel (Collins, 2001), a continuous cycle of providing professional development, following it up with targeted observations, and then working with teachers to use the observations' data to drive the next cycle of professional development.

Care: Caring for teachers includes caring for them professionally and personally. That professional care is a component of growth, but personal care is also critical. Leadership comes with power, and with power comes an ethical obligation to care for the people we hold power over and with. We need to attend to people's health because it is an obligation each of us has to our fellow human beings, and by virtue of having power, we have an increased responsibility to provide care.

The pandemic has shown us people's personal lives have a significant impact on job performance. Add the pressures from external forces which are not directly job-related, such as fractious politics and the case becomes even more clear. If we want to grow our people, we cannot ignore care. **The primary vehicle for caring for teachers is by being present,** which is its own form of care but also creates the opportunities for leaders to learn about other ways to support teachers.

Purpose

Urgent leaders are driven by Quadrants 1 and 3. Intentional leaders think more about where they focus their efforts. **Strategic leaders are driven by purposeful, or Quadrant 2 work.** Strategic leaders understand people are the most important thing in an organization and developing people is inherently work that rests in Quadrant 2.

Let's clarify the distinction between purpose in the Six Dimensions model and purpose in *Strategic Leadership*. The Six Dimensions refer to organizations, but *Strategic Leadership* refers to leaders. In the Six Dimensions model, purpose refers to organizational purpose. In *Strategic Leadership*, purpose refers to the leader's purpose, and the leader's purpose is to support and grow people.

Problems

Urgent leaders treat symptoms. This leads to a temporary easing of the pain, but if the underlying cause of the symptom—the root problem—is not addressed, the symptom will reappear. Because strategic leaders understand this, they look for the underlying causes of misalignment when issues arise.

One of the most important skills for strategic leaders is being able to work with others to diagnose complex problems. We discussed earlier how intentional leaders build systems to help them stay out of Quadrant 3. Strategic leaders take this a step further by identifying root problems as a prerequisite to carrying out change to align the organization to support teachers.

Progress

Urgent leadership focuses on completing tasks, so urgent leaders value action. Strategic leaders are more focused on progress, specifically taking small steps which make situations incrementally better immediately.

Progress can be measured in three dimensions:

1. **Immediacy:** small benefits today are worth bigger benefits down the road.
2. **Simplicity:** simple actions are more likely to be executed with fidelity.
3. **Effort:** simple, small actions which require less effort are more motivating to stakeholders.

By focusing on immediate, incremental changes which are simple to enact, and which move the system into alignment, strategic leaders can slowly, but steadily, improve schools in ways which are less stressful and more enduring for the people within the school.

Strategic Practices

These four principles work together to create a form of leadership which focuses on supporting and growing people. One cornerstone of strategic leadership is the development of the flywheel, a systemic approach to supporting and developing teachers. The other cornerstone is the strategic action cycle, a series of steps and practices strategic leaders use to overcome barriers, identify problems, and sustain consistent incremental improvements.

The flywheel and strategic action cycles are beyond the scope of this guide. We would need another fifty pages and five weeks to learn them. As I said, that's another book and another journey. To conclude this trip, I want to focus you on two concepts and two practices which will help you stay away from the pull of urgency. My hope is you will adopt these practices and use them consistently from this point forward.

Concept 1: M=V/E

Motivation equals value divided by effort (Motivation = Value/Effort). This is an incredibly powerful concept as it completely reframes the "motivation" problem. If people aren't motivated, it means they don't see the promised value as being worth the perceived effort. As a leader, you then have three choices: Increase value, decrease effort, or both. There shouldn't be a need to "rally the troops" or "fire people up." Either we need to do a better job communicating value or decreasing the demand (effort) the request is putting on people. If we can't do either of those things, perhaps the request is not worth following through on.

Any time we think an issue has to do with motivation or effort, we need to look at M=V/E. There are three ways to increase V:

- Help people see how the outcomes will contribute to the person's own goals and/or well-being.
- Deliver a positive result immediately. This is a critical point. A small benefit today may be worth much more than a large benefit three months from now.
- Work for an outcome (V) the participant identified.

There are only two ways to decrease effort:

- Build in supports to make it easier.
- Ask for less.

Think about this: if we look to make a smaller impact which requires less effort, and we can deliver that impact quickly, we have increased value and decreased effort. Therefore, strategic leaders embrace incremental change. Immediate improvements with small efforts equal high motivation.

It's also important to realize different people may have varying V/E ratios for the same initiative. Let's look at two examples. Imagine I'm implementing a new software program to improve formative assessment in reading. For an employee in the twilight of their career, who already has her own successful techniques and who has a relatively low digital IQ, the value is low. They are already successful, so the promised value is small and the effort is high due to technology challenges, resulting in little motivation. That's not a problem with the employee, that's an organizational problem. In contrast, an employee who is a digital native and hasn't developed a method for doing what the software will help with may see a high value and view the change as taking little effort, resulting in a high V:E ratio and high motivation.

> After all, why would we ask someone to do something which will interfere with their productivity?

Concept 2: A-B

A-B refers to the degree of change being implemented. A big change initiative will span from A-Z. Big initiatives take lots of time and require lots of effort. Often, there are no tangible results until a critical benchmark is met, for example, Step G. In such cases we ask people to put in the effort to go from A-G and to postpone any value until the end, thereby equating to $m=v/E$. In contrast, A-B breaks change initiatives into tiny pieces that require little effort and yield immediate improvements resulting in $M=V/e$.

When strategic leaders talk about A-B, they are talking about keeping things small and immediate. Strategic leaders eschew big change (A-Z) and instead embrace baby steps (A-B).

Practice 1: Let the People Decide

This practice is relatively simple to implement but hard to follow. It is hard because it is built on a premise which contradicts what we have been taught to believe. Simply put, teachers should be the ones who identify what they want to focus their growth on. Yes, there are exceptions, but standard practice should embrace teacher-driven PD. This practice is challenging because educational leaders have been taught the following:

1. Teachers resist growth.
2. We are the experts when it comes to teaching.
3. Our job is to use the observation process to determine teachers' growth needs.

The irony is, in many cases, none of these things is true.

Most teachers want better results. They want to have a greater impact and they want more joy from their profession. What they are resistant to is continually escalating demands, frequent changes to curriculum, mandated teaching programs, and incessant testing. Teacher resistance is not about growth, it is about the things which prevent them from doing their core work of supporting and growing students!

Sadly, the second point isn't true either, or at least not universally so. While school administration training programs and district support are becoming better, and principals and assistant principals are developing a deeper understanding of quality teaching practices, we still have a long way to go.

The third point is where the entire premise falls apart. I routinely show a sample lesson of a stereotypical high school social studies teacher lecturing his class. It is a disaster of a lesson at multiple layers. When I ask assistant principals what the teacher should focus on improving first, I get at least three different answers, and the more APs in the room, the more diverse the answers. What's more, there is no single thing which will turn the teacher's class around, yet any single thing would constitute a small improvement. In other words, what we choose to focus on doesn't matter.

Now flip the script. Imagine a conversation with a struggling teacher in which we are fully present. The teacher expresses frustration and disappointment. The teacher appears to be blaming the kids. But we don't jump in. We just listen. After multiple listening sessions, when the teacher knows we listen, we can ask, "If you could make just one thing better, what would that be?" Maybe they want kids to do their homework, or answer questions, or stop calling out in class. It does not matter. We can set ourselves up as servants in helping the teacher focus on the thing which is most important to them.

Now we will tie this back to the previous two concepts. When a teacher identifies an area for improvement, they want to see those results immediately, so we can help focus them on incremental improvements (A-B). Because the goal is their own, it carries a high value (V) and because we are there to support them, the effort (E) is lowered. Providing choice is one way to increase V and support is a way to lower E. Allowing teachers to decide how you can support them increases motivation.

Practice 2: What's the Problem?

Strategic leaders focus on people, and when there are issues, we look to people for the solutions. Every issue exists for a reason. Most issues are created by some sort of misalignment. Remember there are only four problems:

- Structures pose barriers to people's work.
- Resources aren't sufficient to support people's work.

- The purpose isn't clear or runs counter to people's work.
- People lack the knowledge, skills, disposition and or health to do the work.

Again, "the work" is the work of supporting and growing students.

We can combine this understanding of misalignment with the concept of $M=V/E$ to arrive at a simple methodology to help address basic issues:

1. Ask, "Why is this happening?"
   a. If this involves people, ask the people directly.
   b. Gather as many "whys" as you can.
2. Review any information you have and ask why again.
3. Look for imbalances in the V/E equation (v/E) and look for misalignment.

Example 1:

Bettina is consistently late to second period class. Steps:

1. Ask why. Ask Bettina and her teacher, Ms. Pritchard.
   a. Bettina says class doesn't begin until five minutes have passed, and it is a stupid class anyway.
   b. Ms. Pritchard says Bettina is lazy and apathetic.
2. Look at your data. We'll play with a couple different options here:
   a. Bettina is only ever late to 2nd period and Ms. Pritchard does not do anything meaningful in class until five minutes after the bell.
   b. Bettina is only ever late to 2nd period and Ms. Pritchard begins class on time with a bell ringer activity. Ms. Pritchard teaches math and Bettina failed math last year.

    c.   Bettina is late to other classes, but the teachers don't report her.

    d.   Bettina and her boyfriend have been quarreling and her boyfriend's locker is between her first and second period classes. They have been arguing for two weeks, the approximate amount of time Bettina has been late to class.

3.   Look for imbalances:

    a.   In 2a, Bettina sees little value in being to class on time because nothing meaningful is happening. Increasing V is one option. Another option is to lower the value of *being late* by imposing a penalty, such as a detention. However, Bettina isn't late to her other classes, so asking "Why?" again helps us understand that while Bettina's choice to be late is a poor choice, the real problem doesn't lie with Bettina; it lies with Ms. Pritchard. We could increase the value of being in class on time by helping Ms. Pritchard begin class promptly with meaningful activities. Think also about the role of purpose here. The purpose of class is to learn things which will help you in adulthood. If there is no learning going on for the first five minutes, then there is no purpose in being in class.

    b.   In 2b class does begin on time and it is the only class Bettina is late for. We can reasonably conclude Bettina sees math as having a small v and a big E. But it doesn't stop there. Ms. Pritchard has a negative view of Bettina, and may not be doing much to provide support, perhaps making Bettina feel even worse about math. The challenge now is to increase the value of math to Bettina and lower the effort. Remember there are only three ways to increase value:

       • Help people connect outcomes to their own goals. Maybe we can help Bettina see how math, or at least earning a math credit, can help her achieve future goals.

- Deliver immediate positive results. If we could provide support which helped Bettina experience immediate success in math, we could increase the value of math to her.
- Work for an outcome Bettina identifies. This might be possible if Ms. Pritchard used differentiated instruction and included options for student choice.

Also remember there are only two ways to decrease effort:

- Build in supports to ask for less, which would include tutoring, or instructional practices to act as scaffolds. Encouragement and trust also decrease effort because the lower the barrier of fear.
- Ask for less. One way to do this is to focus Bettina on an A-B step. "Bettina, don't worry about the past or what comes next, let's just focus on getting to class on time and completing your homework." Make those two things constitute a win and then move forward from there.

a. In 2c Bettina is late to her other classes as well, but we didn't know because the teachers didn't report it. There is an added structural misalignment here in that teachers are not following policy, but this is a separate issue from Bettina's chronic tardiness. The process will be very similar to what we did for 2a as there seems to be a mismatch between V and E. The fact that it extends beyond one class suggests there is a deeper problem that would call for a more in-depth process.

b. In 2d, the case where Bettina's quarrel with her boyfriend seems to be a major factor, it would be helpful to go back and ask Bettina a few more "whys." Is this a case of value, where Bettina hopes talking to her boyfriend may resolve their relationship, which is far more important than getting to class on time? Or is this an effort issue, where the turmoil of the relationship makes it hard for her to disengage from her boyfriend, even though she wants to get to class on time? Again, we can look at ways to increase the value of getting to math class on time and/or decrease the effort. In any event, helping Bettina learn to deal with conflict in a relationship, and the accompanying emotions, will be a part of the solution because conflict management is one of the problems.

Asking, "Why?" and asking it multiple times is critical. Why is asking why multiple times necessary? Let's go back to our example:

> Asking, "Why?" and asking it multiple times is critical.

"Bettina, why are you tardy to class?"

"Because math is stupid."

"Why is math stupid?"

"I hate it."

"Why do you hate it?"

"I suck at it. I failed math last year."

There are three other important things to pull from this example which are not specifically part of the problem identification process but are crucial to our work as strategic leaders.

First, this example is a case for why strategic leaders focus on people before purpose. When I put purpose first, my focus is on how to get Bettina to math class on time. When I put people first, my focus is on Bettina herself, and what I can do to support her success. Many school leaders already put people first. Supporting and growing people is the reason most of us got into education in the first place, so people before purpose is ingrained in us. The challenge is we work in systems which include structures that try to focus us on purpose, which has become distorted to mean outcomes, which translates into test scores. When I put purpose first, my focus is on how to get Bettina to math class on time. When I put people first, my focus is on Bettina herself, and what I can do to support her success.

Second, applying the simple traditional consequences to this situation are not productive. We can probably use detentions to make the value of being late much lower than the value of being on time, but we have done nothing to increase the value of math class. We have just treated the symptom. Bettina is no better off. We have taken action but made no progress. And because we never got to the problem, symptoms will reoccur. If the problem is Bettina's struggles with math, she is at risk of failing math again because we have not provided support. The more she falls behind, the more likely she is to use inappropriate coping behaviors, because we have done nothing to help her. If the problem lies with Ms. Pritchard and her lack of urgency in beginning class, as well as her low expectations for students, we can expect other students will struggle in her class, which will manifest itself in multiple ways, not the least of which will be unnecessary failures and subsequent dropouts.

This brings us to the third point. We have a bad habit in schools of holding students accountable for teachers' actions. I'm not throwing teachers under the bus, but giving Bettina a detention for being late does nothing to help Ms. Prichard create a better and more effective classroom. Giving elementary school students silent lunch when they were talking in class because the teacher has poor classroom management procedures does not help create a better learning environment for students. It also does nothing to increase the classroom success and thereby make the teacher happier.

When we punish students for adult shortcomings, we are perpetuating the problems, and we are failing *both* students and teachers. The essence of strategic leadership is being able to understand how the small things influence the big things, and to improve people's lives by acting intentionally to improve the small things.

Ultimately, strategic leaders create structures and allocate resources in ways which help them focus on supporting and growing teachers every day. They use their understanding of organizations and people to identify root problems and take incremental steps to improve the situation.

Being able to fully implement strategic leadership is beyond the scope of this guide, but the concepts of M=V/E and A-B, paired with the practices of letting people decide and identifying root problems are enough to keep you moving on your journey.

> The essence of strategic leadership is being able to understand how the small things influence the big things, and to improve people's lives by acting intentionally to improve the small things.

Reflection

Kelli has been able to help Ms. Marple and Ms. Jenna grow. Ms. Marple still struggles with balancing care for her father, her students, and herself, but she now asks for help. She is absent some days, but she is also more prepared, and colleagues have stepped up because Ms. Marple has been more willing to share what is happening and to ask for—and accept—help. Ms. Jenna has made steady improvements in managing her class and her relationships with students has gotten better.

There are still days where Kelli spends too much time on discipline referrals, but she now routinely assesses the reason behind each referral and invests a bit more time uncovering the "why." As a result, Kelli is seeing patterns and connections emerge. She recognizes that some of the school policies aren't getting the desired results, and she's listening more to teachers and hearing how they would like to be supported.

There is still a lot to do, and in some ways the system work is more difficult than the urgent tasks. But Kelli knows that the system work will provide enduring benefits for all stakeholders.

Before moving onto the challenges, reflect on the following:

1. M=V/E fundamentally changes the way we view challenges with people. Think about some previous or current situations where using M=V/E would have changed how you handled the situation.

2. A-B is a simple concept, but many of us tend to make things bigger and more complicated than they need to be. Reflect on times you have tried to go from A-Z instead of A-B.

3. We don't always need to go through a lengthy problem identification process to arrive at the root problem. Simply asking, "Why?" is often enough to lead us to a better response. Think about your recent responses to issues. In which instances would asking "Why?" have provided you with enough insight to make a better decision?

4. This stage is focused on supporting and growing people. Think about how it contrasts with Stage 1 and *Urgent Leadership*. Think about how these different paradigms influence your thoughts, actions, and feelings.

Challenges: Remember the big challenge is required. The other challenges are optional. Do what makes sense given your time, interest, and capacity.

The big challenge

The big challenge this week is:

+ Take a large sticky note. Use a bold marker to write "Why?" Do this with five sticky notes.
+ Post the sticky notes in the following places: Bathroom mirror, computer monitor, on the outside and inside of your office door, next to your office phone, in your calendar/planner or journal.
+ Ask "Why?" incessantly. Why is this happening? Why is this a problem? Why did they respond this way? Why did they say that?
+ As part of asking why, critically examine your assumptions about what constitutes value. For all the expectations we have of our teachers and students, think about the value of each thing we ask them to do. You don't need to act on this, but ask the question: How valuable is this to this specific person?
+ Monitor your thinking and your actions throughout the week.

Optional challenges

1. Provide a list of 5-10 teachers to your instructional leadership team (ILT). Have each member individually write down what they think each teacher needs to focus on to improve. As a team, discuss what each of you wrote. How much agreement is there? If each of you left feedback for the teacher, what should the teacher be working on? What would they be feeling?

2. Conduct some five-minute coaching sessions with 3-5 teachers. At the end of each session, ask, "If you could learn one thing to solve one specific challenge in your class, what would that one thing be?" Do not respond to the answers but reflect on them. What impact would the one thing have on the teacher's

satisfaction and on student learning? Is the one thing something you could help them with?

3. Use the problem identification process on one or two issues that arise. Try it out in your head, but also try using it with others, as a part of a problem-solving session.

4. Monitor the office referrals which come your way and ask "Why?" for each one. Reflect on which issues are more about the teacher than the student. For teacher issues, think about their V/E. Why does the issue exist? What can you do about it?

5. Schedule and attend a Friday afternoon debrief with your accountability partner.

Stage summary

- Strategic leaders:
  - Prioritize people.
    - Support people by increasing organizational alignment.
    - Grow people by building a system supporting professional development cycles.
    - Care for people by being present.
  - Are driven by purposeful, or Quadrant 2 work.
  - Work with others to diagnose complex problems.
  - Create progress through A-B steps leading to immediate incremental improvements.
- $M=V/E$ means that motivation is a direct reflection of the amount of effort required to achieve something of value. The same task may have different V/E ratios for different people.
- A-B represents a very small step to create incremental improvement.
- Teachers should identify what they want to focus their growth on.
- Asking "Why?" is a powerful strategy for uncovering root problems.

Final reflection

The goal of this stage is to help you approach leadership more strategically by providing tools to help you focus on supporting people. Identifying root problems is critical because it leads us to take actions which make things better over the long term. It helps us identify misalignment and guides us in developing supports to decrease effort and providing more immediate outcomes to increase value. As much as strategic leadership is about what we do, it begins with how we think and perceive the people and challenges in front of us.

> As much as strategic leadership is about what we do, it begins with how we think and perceive the people and challenges in front of us.

1. Look back at your to-do lists from Stage 1 and reflect. In what ways are you a different leader today from the one who wrote those lists? Knowing what you know now, how would these lists have looked different? How would your actions have been different?

2. So much of our success as leaders comes down to consistency. Most schools have misaligned elements which pose barriers to leading strategically and putting people first. What are the barriers that might make it difficult to remain strategic? Which individuals can help keep you asking "Why?" and focusing on people, not tasks?

3. Think about the impact you have had on people since you began this adventure. Has your influence increased? Have your relationships changed? Are people behaving differently in and outside of your presence?

Conclusion

Congratulations!

I want to say, "You've made it to the end!" but we both know that isn't true. The leadership journey is never ending, and that is a beautiful thing. But if we aren't celebrating "the end" what are we celebrating?

The journey?

Yes. The goal of this guide is to help you reclaim the purpose of your school leadership journey. The fact that you are here reading the conclusion leads me to believe you have made it—you are back on course!

What's more, you have likely traveled further than you had imagined. In Stages 1 and 2 you've moved from trying to manage time to managing your priorities. In Stages 3 and 4 you've begun to take the people around you on a similar journey as you have talked about and modeled focusing on people instead of tasks, and you've begun to build the infrastructure—the processes and habits—to decrease the time spent in Quadrant 3. In Stage 5 you began reinvesting a precious few extra minutes into your teachers. You amplified the value of those minutes by being fully present. By being present, and by moving into Stage 6, you have begun viewing your school through a systems lens, with the goal of supporting your teachers by bringing it into increasing alignment and creating structures and processes to support consistent teacher growth.

The journey is not complete, but, then again, the leadership journey is never complete. In the end, it really isn't about a destination.

Leadership is about the journey, and more importantly it is about the people we serve along the way. Of all the lessons, this is the one Kelli will hang onto the most tightly. She has learned how moving from tasks to people and being fully present not only help her be a better leader, but they also help her to live better as well. In supporting and growing teachers, Kelli is tapping into the essence of what it means to be human. In connecting with others, she is also connecting to her own deeper search for meaning.

This journey isn't linear. Inevitably, you will find yourself backsliding into the gravitational pull of urgency. It may be how you approach a specific issue, or it might be your entire leadership approach. When you realize you have slipped back into the pull of urgency, don't despair. Revisit this guide. Check your thinking and perspectives. Renew your use of the key practices and move forward. It will become easier each time.

> You are going to be with people.
> You are going to listen to people.
> You can **spend** that time by being only
> partly present, or
> you can **invest** that time by giving others
> the gift of your full presence.
> The amount of time is the same either way,
> but presence is an investment, not a cost.

Here are a few suggestions for anchoring your growth:

1. Remember the first step is to manage your priorities, not your time. Each day, identify your three priorities and make sure one of them is in Quadrant 2. The beauty of this strategy is that it works naturally with the way most leaders operate. We love our

to-do lists. Capitalize on this by making yours a *must-do* list of the three priorities in Quadrants 1 and 3. Consider posting a picture of The Eisenhower Matrix in your workspace.

2. Shift how you describe your use of time:

   a. Differentiate between spending time (on tasks) and investing time (in others). Monitor your own voice and use the language to remind you when you are spending time in Quadrant 3 and investing time in Quadrant 2.

   b. Abandon the phrase "I didn't have time." It isn't true. You have the time, you just prioritized something else. Change "I didn't have time to exercise this morning" to "I chose to stay up late finishing a movie, and as a consequence, chose to sleep in and skip exercise today." This works in the more positive direction as well, as in, "I chose to work with our first-year teachers this afternoon instead of answering email."

These two practices serve two purposes at once. First, they serve as accountability hacks as they force you to own your decisions. Second, they empower you—because they help you remember that you own your decisions.

3. Double down on presence. You are going to be with people. You are going to listen to people. You can *spend* that time by being only partly present, or you can *invest* that time by giving others the gift of your full presence. The amount of time is the same either way, but presence is an investment, not a cost.

4. Share this journey with others. I hope you have already been able to do this, but the more people around you who share the journey from urgent to strategic, the more you can support each other. Imagine sitting down to a meeting about a troubled student and the first questions people ask are about understanding *why*. Imagine an administrative assistant helping put together an SOP for fielding phone calls from upset parents.

Imagine the entire leadership team coordinating schedules, so each member has uninterrupted time each day to plow through necessary but mundane managerial tasks.

Thank you again for allowing me to be part of your journey. If you'd like additional resources to help you continue moving towards being a strategic leader, you can find them on my website at https://www.frederickbuskey.com/. If you would like to share any of your experiences, thoughts, or ideas, please email me at frederick@frederickbuskey.com. I make every effort to read and reply to everyone who writes, and I would love to hear from you.

Cheers,
Frederick

References

Blanchard, K. (2010, September 20). *The Art of Managing Monkeys*. Ken Blanchard. https://www.kenblanchardbooks.com/the-art-of-managing-monkeys/

Bohn, D. and Hollister, S. (2019, September 12). *Google is changing its search algorithm to prioritize original news reporting.* The Verge. https://www.theverge.com/2019/9/12/20863305/google-change-search-algorithm-original-reporting-news-human-raters

Broyles Jr., W. (Writer), Grazer, B. (Producer), Howard, R. (Director), Kluger, J. (Writer), & Lovell, J. (Writer). (1995). *Apollo 13*. Universal Pictures; Imagine Entertainment.

Collins, J. (2001). *Good to great*. Random House Business Books.

Covey, S. R. (1989). *The 7 habits of highly effective people: powerful lessons in personal change*. New York: Simon & Schuster.

Eisenhower, D. D. (1954, August 19). *Address at the Second Assembly of the World Council of Churches, Evanston, Illinois*. The American Presidency Project https://www.presidency.ucsb.edu/node/232572

Sinek, S. (2011). *Start with why*. Penguin Books.

Acknowledgements

During my seventeen years in pk-12 teaching and leadership, I continually struggled to balance what was urgent with what was important. As a teacher of leaders at Western Carolina University and Clemson University, I watched my students—aspiring and future assistant principals, principles, and superintendents—wrestle with the same struggle. In working with them, the pieces of this book slowly came together. Amidst my students' struggles, I would glimpse unique perspectives, meaningful tools, and powerful practices that helped leaders stay true to their purpose. To the students whose patient, creative, and consistent efforts to lead helped create this book, thank you.

I also want to acknowledge the support of my family. In addition to my wife Pam's patient and unwavering support, my four children, Gwen, Lance, Collin, and Mara, have been great teachers and brought meaning to my life that flows through this book. Mara especially has been indispensable as an active accountability partner over the past four years.

There are three mentors without whom I would be a lesser version of myself:

- Dr. Jan Osborn saw in me someone who was kind and wise, long before I merited such faith.
- Dr. Jacque Jacobs taught me to understand the relationship between systems and people, and to serve the latter before the former.

+ Dr. Rob Knoeppel helped me understand what it truly means to put people first by putting me before my work at a time when I was broken and under a shadow.

I want to thank Jimmy Casas at ConnectEDD, not only for his trust and willingness to take a chance, but for his high standards and direct and critical feedback. Throughout this process I have felt that Jimmy wanted this book to be as powerful as I have.

Dr. Robert Maddox, Superintendent of Lexington4 in South Carolina, has been an invaluable supporter, cheerleader, and friend through the entire process.

William D. Parker wrote the foreword to this book. I discovered Will through his podcast, Principal Matters, and his example showed me how someone can have a large influence and yet walk calmly and gently, lifting up others along each step of the journey. Will's easy friendship and servant's heart have been invaluable.

Finally, I want to thank the contributions of those who read the final draft of the book. Each of them offered critical feedback that made the volume you hold in your hands a more powerful guide. It's easy to say, "Good job," but to say, "Good job, *and* here is how to make it better"—that is providing true value. Thank you:

+ Dr. Efraín Martínez, Principal
+ Eleanor McCauley, Principal
+ Dr. Justin Nutter, Superintendent
+ Katie Joiner, Assistant Principal
+ Dr. Sam Sircey, Principal
+ Dr. Heidi Von Dohlen, Associate Professor
+ Maria Werner, Principal

This book will have one author's name on it, but the people and the stories who informed and shaped me are the inspiration for the words.

About the Author

Frederick C. Buskey has been a teacher, coach, and change agent for over 30 years. Most recently, he invested 13 years developing and coordinating training programs for aspiring school leaders at Clemson University (2013-2019) and Western Carolina University (2006-2013). At both schools, he led innovative redesigns of old programs. Frederick has written extensively on leadership development, ethics, and the dark side of leadership, in both scholarly and practitioner journals. His unique blend of scholarly training (EdD in Organizational Leadership from Bowling Green State University), athletic coaching, P-12 teaching and administration (17 years), and public and private sector leadership development (20+ years) provide him with multiple perspectives and insight into the fundamental truths of leadership. Frederick resides among the Blue Ridge Mountains in Cullowhee, North Carolina with his wife and lifelong partner Pam Buskey. Connect with Frederick on LinkedIn at http://www.linkedin.com/in/ strategicleadershipconsulting, through his web site at https://www. frederickbuskey.com/, or by email at frederick@frederickbuskey.com.

More from
ConnectEDD Publishing

Since 2015, ConnectEDD has worked to transform education by empowering educators to become better-equipped to teach, learn, and lead. What started as a small company designed to provide professional learning events for educators has grown to include a variety of services to help educators and administrators address essential challenges. ConnectEDD offers instructional and leadership coaching, professional development workshops focusing on a variety of educational topics, a roster of nationally recognized educator associates who possess hands-on knowledge and experience, educational conferences custom-designed to meet the specific needs of schools, districts, and state/national organizations, and ongoing, personalized support, both virtually and onsite. In 2020, ConnectEDD expanded to include publishing services designed to provide busy educators with books and resources consisting of practical information on a wide variety of teaching, learning, and leadership topics. Please visit us online at connecteddpublishing.com or contact us at: info@connecteddpublishing.com

Recent Publications:

Live Your Excellence: Action Guide by Jimmy Casas

Culturize: Action Guide by Jimmy Casas

Daily Inspiration for Educators: Positive Thoughts for Every Day of the Year by Jimmy Casas

Eyes on Culture: Multiply Excellence in Your School by Emily Paschall

Pause. Breathe. Flourish. Living Your Best Life as an Educator by William D. Parker

L.E.A.R.N.E.R. Finding the True, Good, and Beautiful in Education by Marita Diffenbaugh

Educator Reflection Tips Volume II: Refining Our Practice by Jami Fowler-White

Handle With Care: Managing Difficult Situations in Schools with Dignity and Respect by Jimmy Casas and Joy Kelly

Disruptive Thinking: Preparing Learners for Their Future by Eric Sheninger

Permission to be Great: Increasing Engagement in Your School by Dan Butler

Daily Inspiration for Educators: Positive Thoughts for Every Day of the Year, Volume II by Jimmy Casas

The 6 Literacy Levers: Creating a Community of Readers by Brad Gustafson

The Educator's ATLAS: Your Roadmap to Engagement by Weston Kieschnick

In This Season: Words for the Heart by Todd Nesloney, LaNesha Tabb, Tanner Olson, and Alice Lee

Leading with a Humble Heart: A 40-Day Devotional for Leaders by Zac Bauermaster

Recalibrate the Culture: Our Why...Our Work...Our Values by Jimmy Casas

Creating Curious Classrooms: The Beauty of Questions by Emma Chiappetta

Crafting the Culture: 45 Reflections on What Matters Most by Joe Sanfelippo and Jeffrey Zoul

Improving School Mental Health: The Thriving School Community Solution by Charle Peck and Dr. Cameron Caswell

Building Authenticity: A Blueprint for the Leader Inside You by Todd Nesloney and Tyler Cook

Connecting Through Conversation: A Playbook for Talking with Kids by Erika Bare and Tiffany Burns

The Dream Factory: Designing a Purposeful Life by Mark Trumbo

Stories Behind Stances: Creating Empathy Through Hearing "The Other Side" by Chris Singleton

Happy Eyes: All Things to All People by Ryan Tillman

The Generative Age Artificial Intelligence and the Future of Education by Alana Winnick

Recalibrate the Culture: Action Guide by Jimmy Casas

Leading with PEOPLE: A Six Pillar Framework for Fruitful Leadership by Zac Bauermaster

ConnectEDD
PUBLISHING

www.ingramcontent.com/pod-product-compliance
Lightning Source LLC
Chambersburg PA
CBHW070116030426
42335CB00016B/2175